The Householder's Guide to Plumbing

The Householder's Guide to Plumbing

James M. Haig

revised by M. A. Hewitt

Stanley Paul

London Melbourne Sydney Auckland Johannesburg

Stanley Paul & Co. Ltd

An imprint of the Hutchinson Publishing Group

17–21 Conway Street, London W1P 6JD

Hutchinson Publishing Group (Australia) Pty Ltd
PO Box 496, 16–22 Church Street, Hawthorne, Melbourne,
Victoria 3122
PO Box 151, Broadway, New South Wales 2007

Hutchinson Group (NZ) Ltd
32–34 View Road, PO Box 40-086, Glenfield, Auckland 10

Hutchinson Group (SA) Pty Ltd
PO Box 337, Bergvlei 2012, South Africa

First published 1961
Reprinted 1963
Revised edition 1974
Reprinted 1977, 1979
Revised edition 1984

Set in VIP Times by
D.P. Media Limited, Hitchin, Hertfordshire

Printed and bound in Great Britain by Anchor Brendon Ltd,
Tiptree, Essex

ISBN 0 09 156931 1

Contents

Acknowledgements

The author acknowledges with thanks the help he has received from the Copper, Lead and Zinc Development Associations, the Electrical Association, British Gas Corporation, Marley Plumbing Limited, Wednesbury Tube Company, Le Bas Tube Company Limited and Barking Brassware Company Limited, in the compilation of this book.

J. M. H.

My task was to update this book and I am indebted to the many people, organizations and companies who have so readily provided up-to-date information on latest products and developments, and have allowed me to quote from it and reproduce illustrations in these pages.

All have been particularly helpful and I wish to thank Barking-Grohe, the Electricity Council, Ideal-Standard, Hunter Building Products, Thames Water, the National Water Council, the Department of the Environment, Grundfos Pumps (Technical Department), the Institute of Plumbing and John Hazzlewood, Editor of the IOP journal *Plumbing* for making my task so much easier than I had expected it to be.

M. A. HEWITT

Foreword

This book is intended to help householders to acquire a sound knowledge of the functioning of the plumbing and central heating installations in their homes and enable them to undertake minor repairs and maintenance work. Every householder has a responsibility to his family and the community in being able to control the water and gas services within his home if only because of the safety factors involved. Apart from this he should know that inspection and maintenance can prevent deterioration which could lead to costly repairs and replacements.

The Householder's Guide to Plumbing is also aimed at the potential houseowner; knowing what to look for is all important as so many plumbing faults and inconsistencies are either hidden or virtually inaccessible. Thus anyone intending to purchase a new home should pay particular attention to the arrangement of pipework and the provisioning and positioning of stopvalves, and before making a final acceptance of the property, should closely inspect the surfaces of the bath, washbasin, w.c. pan and kitchen sink.

The materials and appliances used for plumbing and central heating and the skilled labour required to install them are very costly. The extent and complexity of plumbing and heating have also increased with the introduction of more sophisticated appliances and accessories and by the improved standards of living enjoyed by everyone. Particular attention has been given to the increasing use of plastics in plumbing and the development of microbore copper tubes in central heating.

Torbay, Devon   JAMES M. HAIG

The second, revised edition of this work was metricated. This third edition has been brought up to date by further revisions and additions, to ensure that *The Householder's Guide to Plumbing* remains a most valuable guide for apprentices and craftsmen, as well as for the serious do-it-yourself enthusiast.

Thornton Heath, Surrey   M. A. HEWITT

1
Cold-Water Supply Explained

The stopvalve

The plumbing system of a house begins at the stopvalve on the service pipe connecting with the town water main under the road. The stopvalve is the vital keypoint of the water supply to the house. Opened, it admits water to the plumbing system. When closed it isolates the house from the water main. The importance of this control point cannot be over-emphasized when explaining the plumbing system of a house to a householder. In an emergency such as a burst pipe, the speedy operation of the stopvalve could prevent the house from being flooded.

The stopvalve must be accessible. In older-type houses it might be found anywhere – under the pavement outside the house, beneath the path leading to the front door, or it might be in the front garden buried under two feet of earth! If it is in the cellar, unless the householder takes the necessary precautions he may find his path to the stopvalve barred by a mountain of coal – a formidable obstacle to a man in a hurry when a pipe has burst.

In more modern property one might expect to find the stopvalve in a box or pit (or maybe encased by a stoneware drainpipe) between the front gate and the front door. Wherever it is it should be located, made accessible and put in working order. There should be a hinged cover over the stopvalve and when this is opened it will probably be found that by stretching-out full length on the ground, and thrusting an arm down into the depths beneath the cover, it will be possible to touch the stopvalve with the tips of the fingers but not operate it. This is frustrating of course, but the householder should be consoled by the fact that the stopvalve is sufficiently below the ground to be protected from frost. Acrobatic contortions can be avoided by using a simple turnkey which can be made from wood or metal. Two types are illustrated in Figure 1. The turnkey should be readily at hand at all times of the year, having mind to its importance in an emergency.

Figure 1   Simple turnkeys

It is important for the householder to know that the stopvalve closes in a clockwise direction and that great pressure is not required to shut-off the water. The hinged flap of the cover should be kept clean and oiled occasionally. In an emergency the householder will not want to waste time prising open the flap.

Stopvalves

Most byelaws require that:

'Every person who shall lay or use any service pipe shall permit the undertakers to fit thereon a stopvalve enclosed in a covered box or pit of such size as may be reasonably necessary and placed in a position as the undertakers deem most convenient.

Provided that a stopvalve in private premises shall be placed as near as reasonably practicable to the street from which the service pipe enters those premises.'

This means in effect that the water undertaking provides a connection to its water main and installs the service pipe to a convenient point and fits a stopvalve. From there the plumber continues the service pipe into the house.

The correct position of the stopvalve is illustrated in Figure 2.

The service pipe into the house

The service pipe from the house side of the stopvalve should continue at 0.750 m below the surface of the ground until it enters the premises. It is necessary to mention that certain soil conditions cause corrosion of metal pipes. Wet ashes, clinker, red marl clay, wet decomposing matter and wet ironstone have a more or less harmful effect on all metals. Where serious corrosion occurs it is usually due to a combination of poor drainage, high sulphate and/or chloride content of the ground, a prevailing moderate or heavy rainfall on earth of considerable moisture-retaining capacity.

Figure 2
The service pipe to the house

Where corrosive conditions exist it is advisable to afford some protection to the service pipe. The most simple method is to paint the pipe with bitumen, a material both suitable and easy to apply. Alternatively, the pipe can be surrounded to a distance of about 150 mm all round with limestone chippings which have the effect of neutralizing the acidity of the soil.

It has been common practice in the past for the plumber to take the service pipe into the house at a point adjacent to the kitchen sink. This may appear to be a sensible thing to do, considering that a branch is taken from the pipe to serve the cold-water tap over the kitchen sink. Actually, it is bad practice, because no water pipe should be fixed in a position where it can be affected by frost. For this reason pipes should be fixed wherever possible to an inner partition wall, preferably in the warmest part of the kitchen. In Figure 2 it will be seen that the service pipe is taken through a stoneware drain pipe and emerges well away from the perimeter wall.

Service pipes should not be embedded in concrete where this can be avoided. If they must be embedded or be in contact with concrete or cement they should be wrapped with waterproof building paper at the points of contact to allow free movement of the pipe and to prevent the metal from being in direct contact with cement.

It is advisable to 'snake' the service pipe slightly in the trench from the stopvalve to the house. This will provide length to allow for any minor subsidence in the soil.

Stopvalve inside the house

The byelaw states '. . . every service pipe supplying water to any building shall be fitted with a stopvalve inside, and as near as practicable to the point of entry of such pipe into the building'.

There are hundreds of thousands of houses without a stopvalve on the service pipe within the house. To the owners of such houses the key point of the cold-water system remains the stopvalve outside. A stopvalve also fitted inside is an obvious advantage, for if a stopvalve is readily accessible and a drain-off cock is provided immediately above it (Figure 2) the valve may be shut down and the pipe drained at night in inadequately heated dwellings in frosty weather. However, in these days when so many houses are equipped with an effective system of heating, and both pipework and building fabric are properly insulated, it has become a largely superfluous precaution unless the premises are left vacant during winter months.

Drain-off cocks should be provided at the lowest points on all water service pipes within the house to enable the whole, or part, of the system to be emptied so that repairs, alterations or additions to the pipework or fittings may be carried out.

The rising main

The service pipe within the house is usually referred to by plumbers as the rising main. This is because it is the pipe conveying mains water, and it rises up through the house to feed the storage cistern in the roof space.

The rising main provides drinking water and, in some areas, cold water to the bath, washbasin and w.c. cistern. The local byelaws should be consulted because many water undertakings do not permit direct connection of sanitary and ablutionary fitments with main water.

The rising main should be fixed to an internal partition wall, but in many houses it will be found on the inside of the perimeter wall of the kitchen and bathroom, and in some cases will be close to the ventilator in the bathroom or w.c. and right in the line of icy draughts in wintertime.

The wise householder will trace the run of his rising main and take steps to ensure that it is protected from frost. Advice on this subject is given in the section of this book dealing with frost protection.

The storage cistern

The question is often posed 'why must we have a tank in the roof when everything could be supplied from the main?'

First, the difference between a tank and a cistern must be made clear. Far too many plumbers call a cistern a tank and this is both confusing and incorrect.

A *cistern* is a container for water which is under atmospheric pressure (i.e. an open top). A *storage cistern* is any cistern other than a flushing cistern. A *feed cistern* is for supplying cold water to a hot-water apparatus.

A *tank* is a closed container for water under more than atmospheric pressure. The term is used in household plumbing for the hot-water tank (or cylinder).

The container in the roof space of a house is a *storage cistern* and it has a threefold purpose: (i) It provides a reserve of water if for any reason the main supply is cut off. (ii) It limits the pressure of water on pipes and fittings within the house thus reducing noise in the pipes, wastage of water, and enabling pipes of a lighter weight (and less costly) to be used. (iii) It reduces the maximum rate of demand on the company's mains supply.

Further to these points, everyone should know that water undertakers must take the utmost precautions to ensure that the main water supply shall not become contaminated. It is for this reason that some undertakings do not permit mains water to be connected direct to w.c. flushing cisterns, baths, washbasins or to certain types of mixing valves. They fear the possibility of water contamination. There are in fact recorded cases of mains water becoming contaminated by what is technically known as 'back-siphonage', or in simple terms, fouled water being drawn back into the main supply. It is the duty of every householder to co-operate with the water undertakings in preserving the purity of mains water. There may be changes in the Water Byelaws within the next few years which may permit the taking of supplies direct from the main.

The position of the storage cistern

The customary practice is to place the storage cistern in the roof space. There are two points in favour of this: (i) The roof space is the highest part of the house and a cistern fixed there will ensure a good pressure of water at the taps below. This is of particular importance if a shower is to be used in the bathroom. (ii) A cistern can be rather noisy when it is refilling and in the roof space it is more or less out of hearing – and certainly out of sight.

There is an increasing tendency to place the cistern as high as possible but not actually in the roof space. It can be fixed in a cupboard on the landing directly above the hot-water storage tank. The 'head of water' which governs pressure will be reduced, but it will scarcely affect the supply of water at the various taps in the house.

If it is decided to fix the cistern in a cupboard, it should be as high as possible but with a minimum 350-mm space between the top edge of the cistern and the ceiling, or frame of the access door, to permit the cistern to be inspected and cleaned, and the ball valve to be maintained.

The cistern should be supported on strong bearers and base board because when filled with water its weight will be considerable – possibly 150 kg – and should be distributed across as many supporting joists as possible.

The water content will also lower its temperature which, in a warm space, usually above the hot-water storage cylinder, will result in condensation. This can be prevented by lagging the cistern with a 75-mm fibreglass paper-covered wrap, not forgetting the underside and the lid. Never use uncovered fibreglass on open-top storage vessels: should any fibres get into the cistern they can play havoc with ball valve, stopcock and tap seatings and, very often, cause blockages in small-diameter pipes.

For cisterns located in the roof space, ensure adequate bearers and base-board support spanning several joists, and, if possible, locate the cistern over an internal wall. Lofts are usually the coldest spots in a house, especially if insulation has been laid across the joists, preventing heat gain from the warm air below. The loft insulation should be removed from the area under the cistern and the cistern must be lagged as described in the previous paragraph. It is advisable to ensure that gaps around the eaves are filled to prevent through-draughts of icy air in the winter, but take care not to exclude all ventilation, as it is essential in roof spaces.

One factor that is frequently overlooked when lagging cisterns is the overflow pipe, which connects directly from the top of the vessel just above the water line to the outside air. This is the most common cause of freezing of the top of the water in the cistern; when this occurs the ball valve is locked in the shut position and with normal demand the storage will soon be exhausted. To prevent this, fit a bend to the screw-thread of the overflow connection in the inside of the cistern and extend a piece of pipe to just below normal water level so that no cold draught can enter.

Storage cisterns should have rigid and tightly fitting access covers which exclude light and prevent insects, etc., getting into the cistern, but which are not airtight. There must be ventilation.

Capacity of the storage cistern

It is not necessary to lay down any hard and fast rules about the size of the storage cistern except to stress that the water regulations require that they shall conform to the minimum capacity requirements. The local water undertaking should be consulted before a decision is made.

The water requirements of individuals and families differ considerably but it is known that the average daily consumption per head of the population increases yearly and is now probably in the region of 160 litres. This does not mean that these figures should form the basis for calculating the storage cistern capacity for a family, because some members of the household may draw much of their water requirements from sources outside the home such as at their place of work, public buildings and the homes of friends.

The storage cistern refills automatically through the ball valve when water is drawn and it is unlikely that in any home the storage could become exhausted, unless for some reason the main supply was seriously reduced or cut off altogether. There is the odd occasion when the ball valve gets jammed, preventing the incoming supply from entering the cistern but this is very rare indeed.

A cistern with a capacity of from 350 to 500 litres would be sufficient for the average 3-bedroomed house but reference to the water regulations could settle the point.

Remember that the 'actual' capacity of the cistern will be less than the 'nominal' capacity (which is the amount of water the vessel will hold when filled to the brim), because connecting the following necessary pipes to it will not permit you either to fill it to the brim or drain off its entire contents.

Ball valve

The ball valve, usually 15 mm for domestic cisterns, should be fixed as high as possible without perforating any reinforcing rib, and low enough to prevent the ball from hitting the lid when lifting to the 'off' position. The valve should be equipped with a screw-thread adjustment to position the level of the float, rather than bend the arm to achieve the water line. The arm must be of adequate length for the size of the valve and the cistern, and the ball float of suitable diameter. An arm which is too short does not give the correct lift leverage to overcome the pressure of incoming water and may, indeed, submerge the float before lifting suddenly with a concussive effect. This is a common cause of water hammer.

Overflow/warning pipes

It is important to understand the difference between a warning pipe and an overflow.

A warning pipe indicates an overfilling cistern which requires instant attention. It may not necessarily cope with a full-bore-inlet discharge. In an emergency, turn off the control valve and check the valve for sticking. If it is free, get it re-washered without delay.

An overflow should be sized to cope with the full-bore discharge of the inlet pipe. On storage vessels of over 4546 litres' capacity an overflow and a warning pipe must be provided, the warning pipe at the lower level and both discharging where they will be readily seen.

Warning pipe

The top of the warning pipe must be fitted a clear 20 mm below the inlet level of the valve to provide what is termed a 'Type A' air break. This is an essential precaution against back siphonage. Furthermore, this air break must not be bridged by any rigid 'silencer'; that is, silencing tubes of rigid material capable of conducting water back through their lengths must not be fitted to the delivery portion of any ball valve. In the event of a drop in pressure in the feed pipe the contents of the cistern could be siphoned into the rising main, etc. (See section on siphonic action.)

The internal diameter of the warning pipe must be larger than the inlet pipe, with a minimum size of 22 mm and fitted not less than 28 mm above the water line or not less than twice the diameter of the warning pipe, whichever is the greater.

For storage cisterns of under 4546 litres' capacity a
warning pipe only will be fitted, and no other overflow
warning pipe should have as great a fall as practicable,
not less than 1 in 10, and discharge in a position where
readily seen and cause a nuisance, as near the back door of the
house as possible.

When the proposed new Model Water Byelaws are made in 1986,
warning pipes only will be fitted to cisterns of 1000 litres' capacity or
less. Those of over 1000 litres will require both an overflow and a
warning pipe.

Services

Normally at least two pipes will be connected near the bottom of the
cistern: a 'down service', which should be fitted 75 mm above the
bottom, supplying non-drinking cold water to ablutionary fittings;
and a 'cold feed', which should be fitted at a slightly lower level,
some 50 mm above the bottom, supplying water to the hot-water
storage. This is a precautionary measure. In the event of the cold-
water storage being exhausted, the supply at the cold-water taps will
run dry before the hot-water system is affected, thereby avoiding a
possible dangerous situation. If the two pipes in your cistern are at
the same level, screw an elbow on to the down service connection
within the cistern and leave it looking up.

The 50-mm depth of water below the cold-feed connection is to
allow any sediment to collect without affecting the supply to the
taps. Cisterns should be inspected regularly (at least once a year)
and any build-up of deposits cleaned out after first draining the
cistern.

Materials for cisterns

The majority of cisterns installed in dwelling houses all over the
country are manufactured from galvanized iron. These cisterns give
excellent trouble-free service for 25 years and more providing they
are properly installed and protected. They are even better suited for
hard-water districts when a protective coat of lime quickly forms on
the internal surfaces. In very soft water areas the effective life of the
cistern will be less and an asbestos, glass fibre or plastics cistern
would be advisable.

In recent years the development of plastics cisterns has been
rapid and these have many advantages over the other forms.

Polypropylene cisterns have a greater rigidity than those made from polythene but this advantage is not so apparent if the cistern is to be used in an existing house, because it cannot be folded to permit its passage through a restricted trap door into the roof space. This factor is not important of course in new buildings when the cistern can be placed in position before the ceiling and trap door are completed.

Plastics cisterns are made in various sizes all to conform to regulations. They may be rectangular or circular in shape and are very light and easy to handle. They are unaffected by any type of water and of course there are no problems of electrolytic action.

The glass fibre polyester resin cisterns are also gaining popularity. They are non-toxic, stain resistant and have good thermal insulation properties.

It is very important that the manufacturer's instructions be followed when installing plastics cisterns. There have been failures due to wrongful use and from incorrect installation. This applies particularly to cisterns being used to feed hot-water systems. Under certain conditions, some plastics are affected by excessive heat such as very hot water. The plumber is advised to acquaint himself with the performance characteristics of plastics cisterns and order the right one for the job in hand.

All things being equal, there are distinct advantages to be gained by installing a suitable plastics cistern.

Distributing pipes

Distributing pipes convey water from the storage cistern to the various fitments in the house. The definition in the byelaws is: 'any pipe conveying water supplied by the undertakers from a storage cistern or from a hot water apparatus supplied from a feed cistern and under pressure from such cistern.'

The distributing pipe system calls for careful design and correct installation technique. The designer – and the plumber – must consider pipe sizing, avoidance of airlocks, noise transmission, contamination of mains water, protection against frost, corrosion and damage, and of course economy in the use of labour and materials. Unfortunately, the tendency is to take the pipes on the shortest route from the storage cistern to the bathroom, regardless of the fact that it might not be the best route. This is done either from ignorance of the correct principles or to cut down costs – perhaps both.

The protection of pipes required in the byelaws includes the avoidance of water contamination. It is important that the householder should know something about this if he is ever tempted to effect alterations to the plumbing system of his house. There must never be any cross connection between a pipe carrying mains water and any pipe or fitting containing water that is impure or liable to contamination in any way.

Figure 3
Layout of typical household
cold- and hot-water systems

22mm overflow

15mm rising main

22mm vent pipe
22mm cold feed

15mm to w.c. cistern
15mm to basin 22mm to bath

stopcock

22mm

35mm flow pipe

15mm to ground floor w.c. cistern

15mm 15mm to sink

boiler

draincock

35mm

drain cock

stopcock

incoming service pipe

The hazard of water pollution within a plumbing system is a very serious one and is dealt with more fully in the next chapter.

The householder should trace the run of the distributing pipes in his house and identify their purpose. It is customary for one pipe to be taken from the storage cistern to supply the cold water to the bath, washbasin and w.c. cistern – and any other appliances that may be installed. A separate pipe from the storage cistern supplies cold water to the hot-water system and this is known as the cold feed pipe. It is not a distributing pipe in the accepted sense of the term.

A distributing pipe should be controlled by a stopvalve as near as possible to the cistern but in a position where it is easily accessible to the householder. If there is no stopvalve on the pipe then one should be fixed as soon as possible – it might be the means of preventing flooding in the event of a burst pipe.

In Figure 3, the distributing pipes, hot-water installation and rising mains are shown in diagrammatical form.

2
Cold-Water Installation

Preliminary considerations

When water supply is obtained from the mains, the water undertaking's byelaws must be observed, so they should be studied before any work is commenced. The plumber, or whoever is responsible for the installation, must submit details of the proposed work for approval by the water undertaking.

Water undertakings provide printed forms for use by the plumber. These include:

(a) Application for a supply of water.
(b) Request to lay a communication (service) pipe.
(c) Notices that whole or part of the service is complete and ready for inspection by the undertaking.

Form filling and submission should be completed in good time in order to prevent delays in obtaining approval for the work and the supply of water to the premises.

There are occasions when the undertaking may require the supply to be taken through a meter, in which case an agreement will have to be completed by the consumer.

It is important to know that the householder is responsible for any alterations or additions made to the water supply in his house. If work has been installed by a plumber who has not previously notified the water undertaking of what he intended to do and when subsequently inspected it is found not to conform to the undertaking's byelaws it is the householder who will have to foot the bill for such alterations as may be required. The householder should therefore ensure that his plumber has complied with the requirements before allowing him to do the work.

Laying the service pipe

It is usual for the water undertaking to drill the main and lay the service ('communication') pipe, to the stopvalve. The owner of the building pays for this service. When the undertaking permits the plumber to lay the pipe from the main, the actual connection of the ferrule to the main is made by the undertaking, also at the building owner's expense. When the plumber lays the communication pipe from the main he should have it inspected by the undertaking before filling in the trench.

When a house is being built in such a position that it may be necessary to lay a new main or extend an existing main, full details of the house and site should be submitted to the water undertaking as early as possible. The cost of laying or extending the main will be borne by the water undertaking providing the annual income in water rates from the new services to be taken from the mains will be sufficient to reach a prescribed fraction (usually one-eighth) of the total cost. The building owner should be quite clear about his position in this respect well beforehand.

Design considerations

Protection against contamination

The water undertakings of this country do everything within their power to ensure that the supply of water at the household tap is pure and satisfactory for drinking and culinary purposes. It is probable that the water supply in Britain is as good as any in the world. It is of the utmost importance, therefore, that it should not be liable to contamination from any source. There must be no interconnection or cross-connection whatsoever between a pipe or fitting for containing or conveying wholesome water and a pipe or fitting containing impure water, water liable to contamination or of uncertain quality, or water that has been used for any purpose. The provision of reflux or non-return valves is not a permissible substitute for complete absence of connection.

The pipework of the house must be so designed that there is no possibility of backflow towards the source of supply from any cistern or appliance, whether by siphonage or otherwise. All pipework must be made completely watertight and must not be laid through any sewer or drain or manhole nor in ground contaminated by sewage.

Every water inlet to a fixed bath or washbasin must be distinct from, and unconnected with, the outlet. Draw-off taps or ball valves discharging into cisterns or appliances must be fixed so that the outlet of the tap or valve cannot be submerged when the water in the cistern or appliance is at overflowing level. This precaution is to avoid possible contamination by backflow or back-siphonage into the mains water supply.

It is essential that any mixing valves and hot- and cold-water tap assemblies shall be of the type approved by the water undertaking. Attachments fixed to taps or outlets should never be left in such a position that back-siphonage of polluted water into the supply system can occur.

Pipe sizing and discharge rates

Information for determining the size of a pipe for any given purpose is based on the rate of discharge required, the length of the pipe, the head available for loss by friction in that length and the roughness of the internal surface of the piping. This information is available to the plumber in the form of tables, formulae and diagrams, for use in designing water supply. It is necessary to make due allowance to provide against the loss of discharging capacity due to the internal encrustation of the pipes in the course of time.

To keep piping down to a minimum size with a consequent reduction in the cost of installation, the designer must give consideration to layout, and see to it that changes in diameter and direction are gradual rather than abrupt to avoid loss of head. All bends in pipes should be made so as not to diminish materially or alter their cross-sections. The pipes should be as smooth as possible internally, and the methods of jointing be such as to avoid internal roughness and projections at the joints. It might be mentioned here that the effective diameter of a pipe is reduced and severe friction set up if material used for jointing pipes is applied in such a manner that it adheres to the internal surface of the pipe or fitting.

Choice of materials for piping

In choosing the material of the piping and fittings, apart from the character of the water, there are the considerations of cost, appearance, personal preferences and of course the byelaws. The merits of lead, copper, iron and plastics pipes are dealt with in another section of the *Guide*, but it will be as well to mention at this point important facts which must not be overlooked when a final choice is being made.

Apart from repairs to existing plumbing, lead piping must not be used in plumbing pipework installations for water supplies. Until recently it has been held to be a safe material in hard-water areas – because only soft water is plumbo-solvent (capable of dissolving lead) – and the deposit of lime scale formed over a period of time on the inner surface of the pipe prevents contamination.

To a degree, that is still true, but the possibility of unacceptable levels of lead being absorbed by the body through drinking water from lead pipes has led the Department of the Environment, which formulated the Model Water Byelaws for the country, to discourage its use.

Water undertakings make their own byelaws within the framework of the Model Byelaws, though differences may arise because of local conditions. Consequently, water authorities in hard-water areas may, in their byelaws, still admit lead pipes with the qualification that there is no possibility of contamination of the water supply. Clearly the likelihood of electrolysis makes it impossible to give any such assurance. Generally, no lead piping, or lead lining to any storage cistern, should be installed, including extensions or renewal of any existing piping or cistern lining.

Copper, of course, is a popular material, but even here care must be exercised in jointing methods. Pipes supplying water for drinking or cooking must not be jointed by lead-tin solder end-feed fittings. This does not apply to pipes delivering water for other uses.

Copper pipe must not be used to renew any section of an existing lead pipe unless corrosion through electrolytic action is unlikely to occur. It is best to renew the whole run of lead pipe with new copper pipe.

Lead is not the only material frowned upon: wrought iron, mild steel and, in some areas, stainless steel are prohibited by some water undertakings as unsuitable for use with the type of water supplied. Copper can be dissolved by certain waters and, although water containing a small amount of copper may be quite wholesome, it is likely to react to soap by producing green stains.

Electrolytic action

Electrolytic action occurs between dissimilar metals in the presence of moisture – exactly the same principle as a wet battery, and it does, in fact, produce an electric current which will attack the lesser metal. Frequently, the result of such an attack resembles corrosion and many people think it is rust.

It is usually found in the pitting of galvanized iron cist perforation to radiators, etc., when metals are mixed in a system. A common practice has been to paint the inside su..... cold-water storage cisterns with bituminous solution to inhibit this action, but its effect is questionable and, in the event, water authorities now prohibit it because of possible contamination.

Minimum strength of pipes

The byelaws of the water undertakings specify the minimum strength of piping required for service pipes and distributing pipes. It is necessary to comply with byelaws in every case.

Avoidance of airlocks and noise transmission

Good plumbing does not simply happen – it is designed: a fact which, unfortunately, is often disregarded, especially in older-type houses where pipes have to avoid structural obstructions, and bathrooms are not always sited conveniently over kitchens. Ideally, plumbing units should be stacked (placed one over the other) to limit pipe runs and to isolate the noise from fittings as they fill and discharge.

Airlocks are caused by unnecessary high points in pipe runs where air is trapped and the water pressure is insufficient to overcome the build-up of air.

All pipes should be laid with a fall from the highest point (connection to the cold-water storage cistern, etc.) to the drain-off cock at the lowest point. Rising branch pipes to fittings are permissible as air is vented when taps are opened.

Figure 3 shows a typical self-draining self-venting system which will operate trouble-free. Problems arise when branches must travel through floors for any length. If in doubt, remember that a level pipe will both drain and vent.

Services run on wall surfaces should be grouped where possible, lagged and cased and clipped with the type of brackets which will allow for thermal movement. When run across floor joists, allow adequate space in the notchings to accommodate expansion. Copper tube, for instance, will expand only lengthways: it does not increase in diameter. Copper tube in notches that are too tight will squeak every time it heats and cools. Never notch more than 26 mm without seeking the advice of the local authority building inspectors, or you may seriously weaken the floor joists. Do not notch the underside of joists.

Some w.c. cisterns are noisy when filling. As rigid silencing tubes are prohibited, fit either the diaphragm-type ball valve with the collapsible plastic silencing tube which will not pass water back up its length, or a BS ball valve with interchangeable seating, and fit the correct orifice seating for quicker operation.

Probably the most common, and by far the most irritating, noise in any plumbing system is water hammer. Its effect is exactly what the name implies: as though someone were striking the pipe regularly with a hammer. It is caused by the abrupt stopping of a moving column of water, and the primary culprits are worn washers and loose jumpers in stopvalves and taps; or ball valves fitted with float arms that are too short, or floats that are too small.

All stopcocks in rising main supplies must be fitted with fixed jumpers. This effectively stops the chatter that can be set up during the closing of a valve when the pressure on the inlet side may be greater than on the discharge side. The same most definitely applies to cold-water taps to sinks.

Quite apart from the noise, water hammer, if allowed to continue unchecked, can cause pipes to fracture. Any pipe conveying water under a hydraulic head (the height of the cistern above the draw-off – or the mains pressure) is under stress. Water hammer, by creating shock waves, dramatically increases that stress.

Occasionally, excessive pressure from the incoming main may cause problems, and the water authority should be consulted on the type of pressure-reducing valve that may be fitted adjacent to your control stopvalve to remedy this situation.

Excessive pressure can cause the ball valve in the cold-water storage cistern to vibrate, which, in turn, sets up concussion throughout the rising main.

One method of combating water hammer at the ball valve of the storage cistern is to install an air chamber (see Figure 4). An air chamber is formed by a pipe of larger diameter than the service pipe and is fixed in an upright position as shown. As it may have to withstand considerable pressure the air chamber must be strongly constructed and must be airtight.

When the water supply is turned on, air in the chamber is compressed and when a tap is opened the pressure on the air is reduced, and the air is able to expand. When a tap is suddenly closed, instead of the pipe bearing the shock of the water hammer, the air is compressed by the blow and gently expands and contracts until the pressure of the compressed air equals the pressure of the water.

When air chambers are installed the air has to be periodically recharged. This is done by turning off the water supply, draining the pipes, and allowing air into the chamber by opening a tap nearby.

Ball valves sometimes cause water hammer, due to the float being raised and lowered by waves on the surface of the water in the cistern. One remedy is to solder a piece of sheet copper to the bottom of the ball in the form of a flat fin. The fin remains about one inch below the surface of the water and prevents the ball from oscillating.

Figure 4   Preventing 'water hammer'

Planning the pipe runs

All pipes should be so placed that they will not be exposed to accidental damage, and fixed in such positions as to facilitate cleaning and avoid accumulations of dirt. Pipework should be accessible for inspection, replacement and repair. Nobody likes to see pipes and if they can be hidden away so much the better. Providing there is sufficient space to work with the normal tools the plumber can usually arrange his pipes to run through, or adjacent to, cupboards or in recesses. Where pipes are run under floorboards the boards should be fixed with screws to facilitate removal at any time.

Pipes should not be buried in walls or solid floors. There is a tendency to provide ducts or chases for pipework in modern homes. These should be properly constructed to prevent the possible entry of vermin.

If it is necessary for a pipe to run in a wood floor it should, wherever possible, be parallel with the joists. Pipes passing through walls or floors should be sleeved to allow freedom for expansion and contraction and other movement.

Installation precautions

Before any pipe is used for installation work care must be taken to ensure that it is the correct pipe for the job. The pipe must conform to the byelaws with regard to quality and weight.

The pipe should be inspected to see that it is clean internally, and free from particles of sand or soil, metal filings or chips, which, apart from causing obstructions, might well lead to failure by corrosion.

In jointing pipes all internal burrs must be removed and care taken to prevent any jointing material entering the pipes for fear of causing obstruction, corrosion or giving rise to water contamination.

The joints should be cleaned off externally as should any marks made by tools. The screws of holder-bats or other types of pipe fixing should be checked for tightness.

If the sleeves are to be used where the pipes pass through walls they must be slipped over the pipe before it is jointed.

No work should be built-in until it has been fully tested. When testing, care must be taken to eliminate all air from the pipes.

3
Hot-Water Supply Explained

A piped hot-water supply is regarded as essential in every home. There are of course still far too many homes without this modern convenience, but to build a house today without installing a hot-water system of some kind would be unthinkable.

There is more to it than just deciding that a hot-water system should be installed. The system must meet all the hot-water requirements of the household, operate efficiently with the minimum attention and not be too expensive to run. For these reasons a great deal of thought must be given to selection, design and installation.

First considerations

The basic requirement is to provide hot water to the kitchen sink, the bath and washbasin. In large houses there may be washbasins in the bedrooms and downstairs cloakroom and perhaps a second bathroom. Probably the first decision to make is what type of fuel shall be used for heating the water. There are four main fuels, namely, solid fuel, gas, electricity and oil. The decision to use one of these fuels must inevitably be influenced by general considerations as well as preference. How is the house to be heated? That is possibly the first question the plumber will ask the householder. It is obvious that if the fuel used for heating the house can be utilized to heat the water as well this is an economic proposition, hence the great popularity in this country at one time of the boiler at the back of the living-room fire. In fact, although hot-water and heating installation in the home have today become popular topics and have caused the suppliers of fuels and the manufacturers of appliances to seek control of the markets through extensive and costly advertising campaigns, there is still something to commend the simple but properly installed domestic hot-water system comprising a boiler at the back of the fire or behind a purpose built gas-fire, and a tank or cylinder in the linen cupboard. In the winter, with the living-room fire alight all day and every day to heat the room, hot water costs very little. In the summer an electric immersion heater in the storage vessel will provide hot water for most purposes at a reasonable cost.

There is a wide and fascinating choice for the householder today and in the following pages the field of hot-water supply is dealt with.

Planning

Planning is normally determined on a requirement/cost basis and it is as well to bear both in mind when deciding on a hot-water system and the means of heating. As the boiler is the primary concern, let us decide exactly what we are looking for.

(a)   Is it required to heat a room in addition to the water?

(b)   Are you likely to want to add full central heating to the installation at a later date?

(c)   Have you a preference for any type of fuel? If solid fuel or oil, have you space at the side or back of the house to provide the necessary bunker or situate the tank, and is there access for delivery of the fuel? If gas, is mains gas available in or close to the house, or would storage for propane gas be required, and if so, is this feasible and would regulations permit it there?

(d)   Does your property have an integral flue in a suitable position and, if not, have you a suitable external wall to fit a flue?

(e)   Have you adequate wall space to fit the heating unit?

(f)   Is everybody in the family out at business/school during the day?

These points, together with the purchase price of the heater, the fixing price, running costs (including maintenance), efficiency and ease of operation, should be the deciding factors in your choice, as well as some personal factors. For instance, if you are elderly, will you want to hump buckets of solid fuel around in a few years' time?

Efficiency

Boilers are rated for heat output in BTU/hr (British Thermal Units per hour). A BTU is the amount of heat required to raise 1 pound of water through $1°F$. Assuming a 30-gallon storage at $40°F$ is to be heated to $140°F$, the following calculation will give the required rating:

30 gallons × 10 lb per gallon × 100°F temperature rise = 30,000 BTU/hr.

There is a wide choice of high-performance appliances on the market, one of which will suit your specific needs. They include:

1. Independent boilers: gas, oil, solid fuel
2. Back boilers: gas, oil, solid fuel
3. Instantaneous heaters: gas
4. Storage heaters: gas, electric

Only type 2 will provide space heating to the room in which the appliance is sited; the others are designed specifically for the task of heating water. In households where someone is in all day, the solid-fuel boiler with glass front that emits heat to the room can be a comforting companion, but it is essential to obtain the correct grade of fuel as specified by the manufacturer. These boilers can also be connected to a time-clock to increase the rate of burning at pre-determined times.

As an alternative to solid-fuel appliances, a wide variety of gas boilers with separately controlled gas-fire room heaters are on the market.

For business people who are out all day the clock-controlled gas boiler is probably the most convenient and, if no flue is available, the self-contained balanced-flue models can be fixed to most external walls without the need to increase room ventilation for combustion purposes, or to provide piped exhaust. These models draw their own external air supply at the same rate that they discharge waste products.

Instantaneous heaters work on demand from taps, with the advantage that you pay only for the fuel used while hot water is running. The multi-point heater can serve several taps, including showers, but only one draw-off at a time. Single-point heaters (gas or electric) are convenient for sinks and can deliver either through a swivel spout or, if the spout is required to be longer than 0.6 m, can be piped to an open nozzle fitted over a sink. Under no circumstances must they be connected to a tap.

Storage heaters (electric) are heated by immersed elements and are either pre-insulated units or copper cylinders fitted with immersion heaters. These are particularly suitable in properties where it is difficult to site a boiler and cylinder combination; they, and gas heaters, are explained in more detail in Chapters 5 and 6.

Having selected the type of boiler it is next necessary to know exactly what it has got to do. How much hot water does your family require and in what time span? Demands from a family with three teenage daughters each clamouring for a bath, or to wash their hair before going on a date several evenings a week, will differ considerably from those of the household with all boys who follow different sports and want to bathe at different times. Many working wives will want to use the dishwasher and washing machine around the same time, perhaps when husbands want to take a bath.

Clearly everybody cannot do everything at once; it takes time to have a bath, and even washing machines do not draw hot water continuously. Try to assess the peak demand in any one hour and rate your boiler accordingly. Allow 181 litres of water for an average bath, with at least 114 litres of hot water: enough to exhaust a 136-litre cylinder.

Incidentally, it makes good sense to fit a shower. They are very economical, far more so than a bath, and they are refreshing.

Houses with more than one bathroom will require more storage than the average dwelling, but, assuming a typical family of four in a single-bathroom house, a 136-litre storage vessel should be adequate. It is an advantage to fit a boiler with a higher rating than you have calculated as this will speed temperature recovery in times of high demand.

Primary circuits

The hot-water storage vessel (either a tank or a cylinder) is connected to the boiler by means of flow and return pipes (Figure 5) which are known as the primary circuit. The flow is connected from the top of the boiler to the top of the cylinder; the return from the bottom of the cylinder to the bottom of the boiler.

Water heats by convection, a term with which most people are familiar. Water heated in the boiler expands and becomes lighter than cold water, bulk for bulk. Then the colder water in the cylinder, because of its greater density, drops by the force of gravity, displaces the hotter water and pushes it up to the highest point. This process is continued until the thermostat temperature is achieved and the burner or element is shut off, or, in the case of solid fuel, the damper closes down.

The speed at which the water circulates is dependent upon the difference in the temperatures between the flow and return pipes and the height of the cold-water storage tank (which is known as the circulating head). The larger the pipes (28–35 mm), the more water will pass along them quickly and therefore, in a gravity system, the greater the temperature differential. Primary circuits of small-diameter pipes will have a greater loss of circulation velocity through friction.

In Figure 5 imagine that the water in both the boiler and storage vessel is cold. It will be quickly realized that circulation cannot occur because the two columns of water AB (consisting of the flow pipe AC and the boiler itself CB) and DG (consisting of the vessel DE and the return pipe EG) are at the same temperature, have the same weight and thus balance each other.

When heat is applied to the water in the boiler it becomes lighter than the water in the corresponding length FG of the return pipe so that on the whole column DG is heavier than the column AG. The water in the heavier column falls and forces the heated water from the boiler up the flow pipe AC and thus circulation commences. The circulation will continue until both columns are at the same temperature.

Figure 5
The circulation of hot water

It will be seen that the flow and return pipes are connected to the top and the bottom respectively of the boiler. If they were both taken from the top of the boiler it would be uncertain which pipe became the flow and which the return. If both pipes were taken from the bottom of the boiler, no circulation would take place as the heating of the boiler would not put the two columns out of balance.

If both flow and return pipes were taken to the top of the hot-water storage vessel, the hot water would circulate across the top of the vessel and the lower part would remain cold. If both flow and return pipes were taken to the bottom of the storage vessel, the whole of the contents would be ultimately heated, but the entering hot water would mix with the cold water in the vessel and a gradual heating of the whole contents would take place.

When the flow pipe is taken to the top of the hot-water storage vessel and the return pipe from the bottom, as in Figure 5, the hot water from the boiler will tend to remain in a layer on top of the colder water and the depth of the layer will increase until the whole vessel is filled with hot water. The effect is that hot water is available for draw-off from the top of the vessel in the shortest possible time.

Energy conservation

We live in an age of high-priced fuel requiring energy conservation, so systems should be designed to obtain the maximum benefit from the minimum heat input. Very basically, the longer water takes to heat, the more fuel it consumes, because the system is allowing heated water to cool before reaching storage and returning to the boiler.

An efficient system cuts out unnecessary waste, and therefore the cylinder must be placed as close as possible above the boiler. Flow and return pipes should be vertical with a minimum number of bends. Horizontal runs should be avoided, and if this is not possible, kept to the barest minimum and laid with a continued rise to the cylinder. Neither flow nor return pipe should exceed 3 m in length. Other than a safety device and drain-off cock, no valves that can be closed or in any way restrict the bore of the pipe must be fitted to either pipe. Never use elbows to change direction: always bends.

Arrangement

Usually the bathroom is situated above the kitchen. In many modern home improvements it is located beside the kitchen in a back extension, which is particularly convenient for households with physically handicapped or infirm members. Any other room arrangement will involve extended primary circuits so, if possible, should be avoided. Where long flow and returns have to be used, it is a good idea to fit a circulatory pump to the system to speed the circulation. In these circumstances the size of the primaries may be reduced to 28 mm or 22 mm. In practice, 15 mm is too small.

Site the cylinder in an airing cupboard to obtain the benefit of heat given off by the vessel. It should be lagged with an 80-mm-thick insulating jacket to prevent heat loss; but there will still be sufficient warmth to air clothes arranged on slatted shelves. The airing cupboard should be separate from the bathroom, but as close to it as possible.

Pressure

The cold feed from the cold-water storage cistern connects to the cylinder on a tapping some 75 mm from the bottom. It should be at least equal in size to the largest draw-off from the cylinder (22 mm minimum, though preferably 28 mm) and controlled by a gate valve adjacent to the cylinder.

Increasing the size of the cold feed ensures that the hot-water supply taps do not run dry when other taps are turned on. Always connect to the side, near the bottom, of the cylinder or tank and not vertically through the bottom, which can cause turbulence and wasteful mixing of cold water with heated contents. The connection in pre-tapped cylinders is always above the concave bottom to avoid deflection of inlet water. It is essential that incoming cold water is layered at the lower part of the storage vessel.

All gravity installations work under pressure exerted from the storage vessel at the highest point of the system. Apart from pumped supplies head alone gives pressure equal to 9.81 KN/M² for each vertical metre of static water. Therefore, if your cistern is 6 metres above your kitchen tap, the pressure will be 58.84 KN/M² which, when the tap is opened, is converted to velocity, or the speed of flow from the tap. Conversely, if the pipe rises to the floor above, say 3 metres, the pressure will drop accordingly by 3×9.81 KN/M².

The greater the head at the tap, the faster will be the flow of water when the tap is opened. The flow of water from the tap at the washbasin in the upstairs bathroom will be less than that from the ground-floor kitchen-sink tap, which has a greater head of water.

More water will flow from a large tap than a small one because there is less resistance to water flow. The same applies to the piping and fittings leading to the tap. The actual flow of water at the tap thus depends upon the head of water and the resistance (or frictional loss) of the pipes and fittings connecting that tap to the cold-water cistern.

The resistance of a length of pipe or a pipe fitting is not constant. In fact, the resistance increases as the flow of water increases, so that for the same pipe run, a larger flow will mean increased resistance. Conversely, a pipe run of increased resistance will give a proportionately smaller flow for the same head.

The resistance of a pipe is expressed in 'loss of head per metre run of pipe' and, to avoid confusion, the resistance of fittings and the tap itself are calculated to an equivalent length of pipe run and a consequent reduction in the effective hydraulic head.

These calculations are important when deciding on ball valve types (high, medium or low pressure), shower roses fitted at high level on top floors, or in positioning combination hot- and cold-water storage units in self-contained flats.

4
Hot-Water Installation

The basic problem in any domestic hot-water installation is to convert the incoming supply of cold water into a constant supply of hot water at the kitchen sink, bath and washbasin – and to any additional points so required.

The planning stage has already been discussed and in this chapter a typical installation will be discussed, assuming that there will be a combination of a boiler and an electric immersion heater in the hot-water storage vessel. There are a great many variations of this combination but only the basic principles will be explained. The installation will be of the gravity type. An accelerated system combined with space heating by hot water is dealt with in the chapter on 'Smallbore Heating'. Electric water heaters and gas water heaters are also dealt with separately.

Positioning the boiler and cylinder

Having discussed the basic principles, we now come to the practicalities. The sad fact is that the houses in which we live, especially the older ones, are seldom, if ever, designed to allow for the most efficient plumbing system.

Maybe the wife decides on a combination boiler to go in the living room where the family will get the maximum comfort from it. But the bathroom and airing cupboard upstairs are metres away over the kitchen.

The ideal solution is an independent boiler in the kitchen and a gas fire or (if you are going to add central heating) a radiator in the living room. But is there space in the kitchen for a boiler? And what would the effect of the ideal solution be on initial capital cost?

A common reaction is to shrug and bear the inefficient system: but remember your costs in wasted fuel, year after year, will continue as long as the system is in use – and invariably these wasteful running costs are far greater in the long run than the initial expenditure on extra appliances.

Energy is a valuable commodity. This cannot be overstressed. It is likely that in the near future legislation will be introduced to control its use and prevent its waste. Even if it isn't, escalating costs of fuel make it prudent to conserve wherever possible.

If you are saddled with a bad room arrangement, then it may be practical to put the airing cupboard in a bedroom above the boiler. With adequately sized pipes which are well insulated, the noise should be kept below the nuisance level.

Summer heating

Today's gas- and oil-fired boilers can be used winter and summer to provide water heating and this is probably the most economical way to do it. This is not the case, however, with solid fuel. Very few people would care to light the fire during a heat wave to obtain hot water, so the most practical solution is to fit an electric immersion heater to the cylinder.

This is easily enough achieved as cylinders are generally tapped for fitting immersion heaters, but care should be taken against possible back circulation into the primary circuit, which is energy-wasting and expensive.

Back circulation is most prevalent where there are extended horizontal pipes level with the flow entry to the storage vessel. Figure 6 illustrates the point. Water heated in the cylinder can set up single-pipe circulation in the horizontal length A D and reach as far as point E, creating a difference in water densities. The heavier water in the lower part of the storage vessel will move to equalize the pressures, down the return pipe, through the boiler and up the flow.

The speed of this circulation will depend upon the temperature achieved in the top section of the cylinder. It will never be rapid, but any significant water movement which transfers heat to the lower part of the system is energy-wasting.

This situation can be prevented by good design, but the reader must appreciate that it is impossible to detail here remedies for the countless existing systems which may suffer from this fault. However, the following are the basic principles, which should be applied in every new installation and adapted wherever possible to suit those that are existing.

Ensure that the flow pipe connecting to the upper part of the body of the cylinder is vertical for its full height and as close as practicable to the cylinder.

connection of flow and return pipes

Figure 6
Connection of flow
and return pipes

Set the temperature control on the thermostat to a maximum of 60°C. Excessively hot water in the cylinder may not only affect the temperature of the cold flow pipe, but will also cause precipitation of lime scale in hard-water areas.

Do *not* be tempted to fit valves to the primary circuit to control any back circulation as it will prove very dangerous if they are forgotten and left shut when the boiler is lit for the winter season.

Furring

In hard-water districts, furring of flow and return pipes, the boiler (which, incidentally, holds only a few pints of water) and the cylinder can be a major problem. It is caused by water depositing what is termed its temporary hardness, a mineral held in suspension by the water until the temperature exceeds approximately 71°C. A common deposit is lime scale, which quickly coats the walls of the boiler, pipes and, to a lesser extent, the storage vessel.

The greater the mineral content of the water, and the higher the operating temperature, the quicker the boiler and pipes will fur up. There have been instances where systems have ceased to work because boilers have been so clogged with lime that there was less than a quarter of a pint of water in the jackets.

Not only does this prevent circulation, it also effectively insulates the heat-exchange surfaces which, again, is fuel-wasting. For proper efficiency and economy these deposits must be avoided. Many households install water softeners (which are dealt with in Chapter 19) which are an ideal solution if you want the benefit of softened water for all purposes. If your only concern is the hot-water system, then the cure can be quite simply effected by asking your plumber to fit a calorifier instead of the customary direct cylinder.

Calorifier

The calorifier, or indirect cylinder, is a cylinder with an internal heating coil, or tank. The flow and return pipes from the boiler connect to the internal coil which, in turn, heats the water in the outer cylinder.

Figure 7   *Calorifier
              (or indirect
               cylinder)*

As this inner tank, or coil, is entirely self-contained and provided with its own separate cold feed and vent (to a separate feed and expansion tank), and there are no draw-off points on the primary

circuit (other than the drain-off valve), the same water is
constantly. Consequently there is only the initial deposit
ary hardness and, providing the system is not drained do
reason, it will function indefinitely with only the loss from evaporation to be made up from the feed and expansion tank.

This method of heating is very efficient and provides rapid temperature recovery to main hot storage as replacement cold water
does not enter the boiler every time hot water is drawn off.

Vent pipe

A vent pipe must be taken from the top of the storage vessel and
discharged above the cold feed cistern. Its purpose is to permit the
discharge or escape of any air or steam in the system.

Figure 8
Vent and feed pipes

This pipe is often wrongfully described as the expansion pipe on
the assumption that the expansion of the water in the system when it
is heated will be taken up by this pipe and, if necessary, expelled into
the cold feed cistern. In point of fact this is not true because the
expansion takes place in the cold feed pipe. Reference to Figure 8
will show that in order for water to be discharged from the vent pipe
it would have to be lifted the distance AB above the level of the
water in the cold feed cistern. The fact that the vent pipe will be hot
and the cold feed pipe cold will only account for a difference of
about 12 mm/300 mm of vertical distance between cold-water
cistern and hot storage vessel. It is important that the vertical
distance between the free surface of the cold water in the cistern and
the turn-over of the vent pipe is greater than 12 mm/300 mm of
vertical distance between cistern and storage vessel, as otherwise
discharge of hot water via the vent pipe into the cold-water cistern
will be liable to take place. The end of the vent pipe must not dip

into the cold water in the cistern as otherwise siphonic action might feed cold water via the vent pipe to the top of the storage vessel.

Draw-off piping

The hot-water supplies to the various taps are taken from the vent pipe as close to the top of the cylinder as possible. This branch is the 'high' point of the hot-water service and the distributing pipes should be laid with a constant fall away, although where they run on skirting boards or under floors in joists they may be level.

As previously stated, the storage vessel should be sited as close as possible to the various points to be served. Overlong runs mean that a considerable quantity of cold water must be drawn from the tap before the hot water arrives. Then, when the tap is turned off for any length of time, the hot water in the pipe will in turn cool, wasting the heat used to warm it. These long runs of pipes are known as 'dead legs' and because they waste energy they must be avoided.

The maximum lengths of pipe permitted under byelaws for supplying hot-water draw-off taps are: up to 19 mm diameter, 12.0 m; over 19 mm and up to 25 mm diameter, 7.6 m; over 25 mm diameter, 3.0 m.

For a common pipe run reducing through several sizes the length is determined by the largest diameter.

Clearly it is important to plan pipe routes. A basin and bath within 7.6 m of the cylinder can be supplied from a 22-mm pipe and the sink tap also if it is within the overall pipe length. Some plumbers advocate increasing the diameter of the initial length to the bath to 28 mm to avoid possible starvation at the sink if both taps are used at the same time. This is an unnecessary precaution and limits drastically the permitted length of run.

Figure 9A is a fairly typical example of pipe arrangement where importance is attached to running pipes in corners of walls for concealment in casing; possibly pleasing to the eye, but likely to prove inefficient. A better arrangement is shown in Figure 9B.

Full-way gate valves should be fitted to branch supply pipes as close as possible to, but without obstructing, the open vent. This ensures control of the entire lengths of pipework for maintenance purposes. *Under no circumstances must a valve be fitted to the open vent.*

We have dealt with supplies to basic amenities, but these days households will probably have a plumbed-in washing machine, perhaps a dishwasher, and in many bathrooms a bidet.

Hot-water supplies to washing machines and dishwashers may be taken from the supply to the sink and terminated at hose-union taps. These not only control the supply of water to the machines but provide suitable connections for the flexible hose with which these machines are invariably equipped. Cold-water supplies to these machines should be from the storage tank and also terminated with a hose-union tap.

Figure 9
Draw-off piping

It is likely to be a requirement in the very near future for all such machines to include a suitable integral anti-backflow device. A hosepipe must not be connected permanently to a water service pipe.

Bidets

Spray nozzles fitted in the bottoms of bidets must be supplied by a separate branch pipe from the vertical open vent pipe above the cylinder and be exclusive to that bidet. Cold-water connection to submersible spray nozzles in bidets must be taken separately from the cold-water storage cistern and be exclusive to that bidet.

These fittings must not be connected to a mains water supply.

In general, all hot-water pipes should be lagged to prevent heat loss. Control valves should be of the 'gate' type. If screw-down stopcocks are used they should have fixed jumpers and washers suitable for operating temperatures. Draw-off cocks must be provided at the lowest point of all branches.

Secondary circuit

The necessity of locating the storage cylinder as near as possible to the draw-off points and within the limit for 'dead leg' branches has been stressed.

Sometimes, however, this is just not possible. In these cases a secondary flow and return which provides a circulation from the vertical vent to a point near the draw-off, and returns to the cylinder, solves the problem. The dead leg is then measured from the return connection to the secondary flow to the draw-off point. This arrangement is suitable only for boiler-fired systems and should not be incorporated in a system designed to be heated by electricity.

The secondary flow pipe (see Figure 10) should fall slightly all the way from the vent and the return back to the cylinder and connect within the top third of the storage vessel (tappings are provided for this connection on calorifiers and also on direct cylinders if ordered). If connected any lower, the water within the tank may be cooler than that in the return and thus, because of its greater density, prevent the return water from entering the cylinder and so stop the circulation.

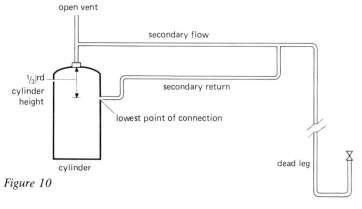

Figure 10

Pipe sizing

Pipe sizing and flow rates are a complex subject, too involved to discuss here in basic terms. However, if you are planning additions to your plumbing system it is necessary to know if they will work. Purely for guidance, the following table illustrates the number of smaller-diameter pipes that may be supplied by a larger-diameter pipe in a domestic household, providing a suitable head pressure exists.

	Taps			
Pipes	35 mm	28 mm	22 mm	15 mm
35 mm	1	2	4	10
28 mm		1	2	6
22 mm			1	3
15 mm				1

As shown, a 28-mm cold-water down-service pipe will serve two 22-mm taps or six 15-mm taps. Three 15-mm taps may be connected to a 22-mm pipe.

Remember that the simultaneous use of two taps in the average house is reasonably rare, while three at the same time is very unlikely.

All that now remains to complete the installation is to fit the electric heater. This may be a horizontal immersion heater, a vertical circulator or even twin elements like the 'two-in-one' heater. It should not be forgotten that the effective hot storage capacity is that above the level of a horizontal heater or above the level of the bottom of a circulator, and that no part of a heater should be below the level of the cold feed.

In the case of a horizontal immersion heater, sufficient space between the heater and the bottom of the vessel must be allowed for the accumulation of scale and sludge.

If all the foregoing points are attended to, a simple straightforward solid-fuel/electric system will result and, providing the hot storage vessel is properly insulated with 75 mm of approved insulating material, the standing losses will be not more than between one and one and a half units a day.

Such a system can be left switched on continuously under thermostatic control, and the full benefit of constant hot water on tap be experienced, without excessive running costs.

Sealed primary hot-water systems

The Standing Technical Committee on Water Regulations has produced proposals for new Model Water Byelaws which, if approved, may permit the installation of unvented hot-water systems in the UK. They are expected to come into operation in 1986.

It is important that any such permitted system should be installed only by fully qualified plumbers. Prospective users should consult the local water undertaking for approval before ordering any such system and should consult the Institute of Plumbing for a list of Registered Plumbers in their area.

Readers are strongly advised not to respond to letterbox advertising for this or any other plumbing or heating job. Unvented systems may be dangerous if they are not correctly designed and installed, with all the right controls in the right places.

In the unvented system, water is subjected to a higher pressure and will boil at a higher temperature. If something goes wrong with the safety devices built in to allow steam or water to escape, pressure in the hot-water cylinder quickly rises until the cylinder can no longer contain the steam or hot-water pressure and explodes. The safety of the unvented system depends on the totally reliable functioning of all its mechanical controls, at all times, so they must be correctly selected and installed.

Unvented systems are widely used, indeed are the norm, in other countries, and the safety record in those countries is good. But we are not experienced or familiar with them in the UK, so it is important to employ only plumbers who have been soundly trained in their design and installation.

5

Electric Water Heaters

In general there are two types of electric water heater: (1) the self-contained type consisting of storage cylinder, heating element, thermostat and pipe connections, together with thermal insulation and outer case; and (2) the immersion heater or circulator consisting of a heating element and thermostat for fixing into an existing hot storage vessel.

It should be understood that the heating element is common to both types, so that the following information on heating elements applies generally. In the self-contained electric water heater the positions of the heating element and thermostat are fixed by the manufacturer, but the immersion heater or circulator can be fixed in any desired position.

Electric heating elements

The heating or resistance wire in electric heating elements is almost invariably of nickel-chromium. There are two main types of elements distinguished by the fact that while one type can be withdrawn without the necessity for emptying the storage vessel, the other type cannot be removed without breaking a water joint.

The withdrawable type usually consists of a spiral of resistance wire mounted on a ceramic insulating former, the whole being inserted in a copper sheathing tube. In the other type the resistance wire is solidly embedded in a compressed insulating material within a flat blade or tubular sheath. The tubular sheathed variety usually employs a sheathing tube of about 12-mm diameter and can be bent or formed to almost any shape.

Loading

The water heating elements that will be encountered in the water heating systems of the small house usually have loadings ranging from 500 to 3000 watts according to requirements.

Heating surface

If it were possible to keep the heating surface of the water heating element free from scale, a very high loading of heating surface would be possible. In certain hard-water districts, however, where the heater may become covered with scale, a loading density that would otherwise be quite satisfactory will result in the surface temperature of the element sheathing becoming dangerously high, so high in fact that it may exceed the melting point of the tin with which the sheaths are usually coated. The scale does not decrease the efficiency of the heater – with electricity the output of heat must be proportional to the input of electricity – but it does obstruct the transfer of heat from element to water and thus leads to a building-up of the temperature of both element-sheath and resistance wire. Excessive sheath temperatures result in conditions favourable to corrosion of the sheath whilst excessive resistance wire temperatures lead to danger of wire failing by burning out.

The watts density may be as high as 50 watts/645 mm² in the case of the tubular sheathed variety, but usually lies between 10 and 30 watts/645 mm² in the case of the withdrawable type.

Self-descaling elements

The usual shape of sheathed tube type of element shown in Figure 11 is such that its expansion and contraction during heating and cooling is sufficient to fracture and throw off some, if not all, of the deposit of scale. Ample space round and below the element should be allowed for the accumulation of scale which may, with certain kinds of water, fall off in large flakes.

Action of water on the sheathing metal

Sheaths are usually made of copper and, as certain kinds of water are capable of dissolving copper, are usually tinned in order to prevent such action.

In hard-water areas, the scale, as it is shed from the element by expansion and contraction, often takes off the tin with it, and in time the element may be completely de-tinned. Such action is hastened by overheating and softening of the tin coating.

The life of a heating element depends very largely upon the type of scale that is formed, and it is consequently advisable to take advantage of the local experience of the Electricity Board in deciding the type of heater to use in any particular area.

Figure 11   Immersion heater

removable element

tubular type mineral
insulated element

non-removable

Thermostats

The type of thermostat used in water heating is of quite simple design. It consists of a tube and rod of metals having different thermal coefficients of expansion, and the relative movement of these two pieces of metal is made to operate the switch portion of the instrument.

Thermostats should comply with the appropriate BS DESIGN: Section 2B, and must be of suitable capacity to deal with the loading of the heating element.

Where the supply of electricity is AC, by far the greater majority of thermostats have micro-gap contacts with some kind of device which gives the contacts a quick 'make and break' action.

In breaking the circuit the contacts are moved only a very short distance apart, hence the term 'micro-gap'. This distance in itself is not sufficient to extinguish the arc that is set up as the circuit is broken. The extinguishing of the arc is done automatically by the alternations of the supply when the pressure during the cycle reaches zero; this happens 100 times a second. The contacts themselves are relatively large in size and thus cool the arc to such an extent that it is prevented from re-striking when the voltage reaches its maximum figure again.

The micro-gap thermostat is sometimes used on a DC supply with a condenser of one or two microfarads' capacity connected across the contacts, but this practice is not recommended by the makers.

Another type of thermostat which is sometimes employed makes use of a mercury tube which is tilted by the action of the bimetallic rod; the mercury in the tube making and breaking contact.

Mercury tube thermostats are suitable for either AC or DC but are not so compact in size as the micro-gap type and must, of course, be installed the proper way up and be in correct alignment.

Thermostat differential

The word 'differential' is used to describe the number of degrees between the temperature at which a thermostat switches the supply off and the temperature at which it switches it on again. Other things being equal the differential depends upon the length of the thermostat stem. Common values are from 5 to 10°C for lengths up to 300 mm and 3 to 5°C for longer stems. The effect of a deposit of scale on a thermostat is to widen the differential.

There is no particular object in having a very small differential in water heating as there is no need for the temperature to be controlled very precisely. It will, of course, be appreciated that the smaller the differential, the more frequently the heating element will be switched on and off. On the other hand, if the differential is too large the temperature of the water when drawn off just before the thermostat is due to cut in will be unduly low and the output of hot water will thus be reduced.

A thermostat is affected by the average temperature of the whole of its operating length and thermostats that are fitted horizontally in hot-water vessels function rather differently from those that are fitted vertically.

If a long thermostat which extends practically the whole length of a storage vessel is fitted vertically, the temperature at which it operates will be in effect the average temperature of the water in the vessel. A short thermostat fitted vertically will be affected only by the water in the lower or upper half of the vessel, depending upon whether the thermostat is fitted from the top or the bottom. Consequently, with vertical fixing, the longest thermostat that can be accommodated is the best in every case.

If small quantities of hot water are drawn off at frequent intervals from a storage vessel fitted with a vertical thermostat, it is quite possible for the water at the top of the vessel to be boiling, although the mean temperature, which is the temperature that affects the thermostat, is lower than the temperature for which it is set.

When the thermostat is fixed horizontally, it will obviously be affected only by the temperature of the layer of water with which it is surrounded. If used as it normally will be with a horizontally fixed heating element, it will operate as soon as the temperature of the body of water above its own level reaches the cut-out temperature because the horizontal arrangement of the heater tends gradually to raise the temperature of the whole body of water above its level. It will thus be seen that the temperature marked on the dial of a thermostat will be approximately correct if the thermostat is fixed horizontally in conjunction with a horizontal heating element, but if it is fixed vertically the temperature of the water at the top of the vessel will probably be in excess of that shown on the dial.

The setting of a thermostat should always be checked before any installation is handed over owing to the possibility of the instrument having been damaged during transit. In hard-water districts the thermostat setting should not exceed 60°C. Higher settings are permissible in soft-water districts, but the setting should not be higher than is necessary to ensure a satisfactory supply of hot water, in order to avoid unnecessary heat losses.

Position of the heating elements

Heating elements may be fitted in three different positions in the hot-water storage vessel, i.e.:

(a) Horizontally through the side.
(b) Vertically through the top.
(c) Vertically through the bottom.

In each case the heating element is fitted internally into the storage vessel and the amount of heat actually transferred to the water will be the same however it is fitted. There will, however, be a considerable variation in the way in which the water is heated and in the temperature of the water at various levels in the vessel.

Horizontal entry

If the heating element is fixed horizontally from the side (see Figure 12A) there will be a tolerably rapid and general circulation of the water within the vessel, with the result that in a given time a large volume of water is heated through a small number of degrees. This means that there will be a relatively small difference in temperature

between the top and bottom of the vessel and there will be a
tendency for the whole content of the vessel to be gradually heated.
Water that is below the level of the heating element will remain
practically unheated and consequently the heater should be fixed
low down in the vessel.

With this arrangement of heating element, it is usual for the
thermostat to be fixed horizontally and slightly above the level of
the heating element. When in this position it will switch off the
heating element as soon as the layer of water in which it is fixed
reaches the temperature for which it is set.

When the heating element is cut out, the temperature of the water
at the top of the vessel will be slightly higher than the cut-out
temperature, and the layer of water between the level of the heating
element and that of the thermostat will be at a slightly lower
temperature.

circulation with element fixed
horizontally

circulation with element
fixed vertically from
the top

A

B

Figure 12   Position of elements

The water below the heating element will be practically unheated
and it would be clearly useless to fix the thermostat below the level
of the heater.

The mounting of the heating element and thermostat in one head
simplifies fixing because only one hole in the storage vessel has to be
provided and in practice this arrangement is satisfactory.

Vertical top entry

If the heating element is fixed vertically from the top as in Figure
12B it must be long enough to extend sufficiently far downwards to

heat the required volume of water, as water below the level of the heater will not be heated. In this case, the water heated by the element rises vertically and as it will be in contact with the heater all the way to the top, it is obvious that each portion of the element will heat still further the ascending column of hot water. This means that a relatively small quantity of water is in circulation and that this small quantity of water will absorb the whole output of the heating element with the result that hot water will collect in a layer at the top of the storage vessel, there being a considerable temperature difference between the water at the top and bottom of the vessel.

As time goes on the depth of the layer of hot water increases until the whole of the water above the level of the bottom of the heater is heated. It is thus seen that by this method of fixing, a small quantity of hot water is obtained in a relatively short space of time.

When the heating element is fixed vertically from the top it is usual for the thermostat to be fixed in the same position, and the length of the thermostat should be proportional to the length of the heating element. If the length of the thermostat is much shorter than the heating element, the heating element will be switched off before the water below the level of the thermostat is fully heated.

The thermostat will cut out when the average temperature of the water surrounding it reaches the cut-out temperature, and a high temperature at the top end of the thermostat will be counteracted by a low temperature at the bottom.

Vertical bottom entry

If the heater is fitted vertically from the bottom of the vessel, the way in which the water is heated will be a compromise between horizontal fixing and vertical fixing from the top. If the heating element is long and extends nearly to the top of the vessel there will be little difference between this arrangement and vertical top entry. On the other hand, if the heating element is short and does not extend far above the bottom of the vessel, the heating effect will not be very different from that of the horizontal arrangement except that there will be rather more tendency for a layer of hot water to be formed at the top of the vessel.

As in other cases the thermostat will normally be placed in the same position as the heating element and should be as long as possible. If the thermostat is very short, drawing off a relatively small quantity of water will cause the thermostat to cut in and it is possible that the amount of heat added to the water before the thermostat cuts out again will exceed the amount of heat in the water drawn off. If this is so, continual drawing of small quantities of hot water will gradually build up the temperature at the top of the vessel and may lead to boiling.

Self-contained water heaters

The term 'self-contained' is used to distinguish the complete factory-made assembly of vessel, heater and thermostat together with its insulation and outer case from the installation where an immersion heater or circulator is fixed on site into an ordinary hot storage vessel that is usually part of an existing solid-fuel hot-water supply system.

Self-contained electric water heaters should comply with BS 3456, Section A13, and BS 843 which lays down details of size, performance, and screwed connections for piping.

It is advisable to consult the attractive technical literature issued by manufacturers of water heaters before deciding on the type to use for any specific purpose.

Self-contained electric water heaters can be classified broadly as:

(a) 'Non-pressure' or 'open outlet'-type which are controlled from the inlet side and supply one point only.

(b) 'Pressure'-type heaters which will work under pressure from a feed cistern and are intended to supply one or more taps.

(c) Cistern-type water heaters incorporating a self-contained cold-water cistern arranged for direct connection to the cold-water main and serving one or more taps.

(d) Two-in-one water heaters provided with two heating elements and serving one or more taps. This type is designed primarily for installation in close proximity to the kitchen sink.

Non-pressure type heaters

Non-pressure type heaters are fitted with open outlets and have the controlling tap on the inlet side so that they may be connected directly to the cold-water mains.

The top of the container is usually vented with the double object of preventing pressure building up should the outlet become obstructed, possibly by scale, and of preventing the formation of a vacuum through the action of the draw-off pipe. Figure 13 shows a typical 'open outlet' sink heater incorporating an anti-siphonic cold-water inlet pipe which prevents the contents of the vessel being drawn back into the cold-water mains.

Figure 13   Open outlet sink heater

As water expands approximately 4 per cent in volume when heated through a temperature rise of 80°C, dripping will take place from the open outlet of a non-pressure type heater unless some means are employed to prevent it.

Various forms of anti-drip devices are employed, one being a siphonic trap formed at the top of the outlet pipe as in Figure 14, so that when the tap is turned off, the level of the water in the container drops slightly to allow for subsequent expansion without dripping from the outlet. This, of course, means that when the tap is turned on there will be a slight delay before water flows from the heater and that water will continue to flow for a short time after the tap is closed.

siphonic action broken at this point

level of water flowing

anti-drip device

level of water after expansion

level of water after draw off

water level lowered to this point by siphon when water inflow stops

stand pipe

hot water outlet

cold water inlet

Figure 14
Anti-drip device

The satisfactory working of such a device depends to a great extent upon the flow of water being maintained at a constant figure and consequently it is usual for a restricting device to be fitted to the inlet tap.

Some water authorities insist on a siphonic anti-drip device being provided, but others who recognize the fact that with the siphonic

water level

bell mouth top to stand pipe

stand pipe

Figure 15
Water heater with air seal outlet

baffle

inlet valve

spout outlet

air sealed outlet holding column of water in stand pipe

anti-drip device the user cannot draw very small quantities of water from the heater and that the siphon is apt to become choked with scale in hard-water districts, permit single-point heaters to be connected provided that they have an air seal fitted to the end of the spout as in Figure 15. This type of heater has a clear waterway at the top of the standpipe and, in action, is completely filled with water up to the spout. The construction of the air seal keeps air from ascending the standpipe and thus prevents displacement of the water.

Another design is made with the ejector device shown in Figure 16 which consists of an anti-drip chamber inside the heater adjacent to the cold-water inlet. When at rest this chamber is filled with water approximately equal in content to the expansion of the whole of the water in the cistern. When the inlet valve is open, the incoming water exerts a suction upon the contents of the chamber and empties it. When the inlet valve is closed, the water in the heater finds its way back by gravity into the chamber which, when filled, reduces the level of the water in the heater well below the standpipe. It is

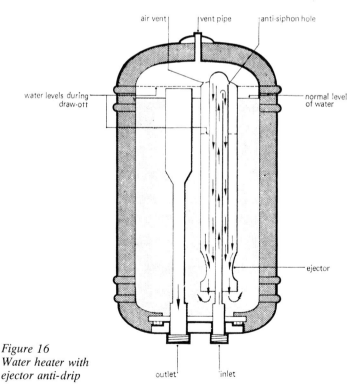

Figure 16
Water heater with
ejector anti-drip

impossible, therefore, for the water heater to drip, provided the waterways to and from the anti-drip chamber remain clear. As the water in this part of the heater is comparatively low in temperature, there is little danger of scaling even when hard water is used.

Pressure-type heaters

Pressure-type heaters are designed to work under the head from a cold-water feed cistern at high level provided this does not exceed 18 m and to supply any normal number of taps.

Figure 17 shows a typical pressure-type heater. The smallest multipoint heater in general use is the 55-litre size in view of the fact that this is the smallest size capable of giving one bath.

Pressure-type water heaters are controlled from the outlet side and, consequently, no anti-drip device is required.

Figure 17   Pressure-type water heater

Cistern-type water heaters

These heaters are also suitable for supplying any normal number of taps. They consist essentially of a pressure-type heater fitted with a ball-valve feed cistern at the top of its casing. A cistern-type heater therefore forms a complete hot-water system in itself, needing no external vent pipe and being suitable, subject to the water authority's requirements, for direct connection to the main. It must, however, be fixed above the level of the highest tap which it has to supply. Owing to the internal pressure being limited to the small head of water provided by the feed cistern, the storage vessel can be made in rectangular shape, thus reducing the projection from the wall, a useful feature where space is limited.

Figure 18   Cistern-type water heater

There are two types of cistern heater:

(a) Constant volume and varying temperature type.
(b) Constant temperature and varying volume type.

The first, shown in Figure 18, operates in precisely the same way as a pressure type heater.

The second type works on the principle of restricting the flow of cold water into the heater to an amount that can be heated immediately to whatever storage temperature is desired or, in other words, by heating the water to the required temperature as it is admitted. The stored hot water is obtained not by displacement by cold water but by emptying the storage vessel so that the water level in the vessel falls as water is drawn off. With this type of heater the draw-off pipe is taken from the bottom of the storage vessel. Such heaters must be designed so that the heating element is always

Figure 19   Cistern-type water heater

surrounded with water and an arrangement whereby this can be done without reducing the useful storage capacity of the vessel is shown in Figure 19. The heating element is housed in an inner chamber arranged in such a way that the chamber remains full of water whatever the level of the water in the storage vessel itself. This type of heater never runs cold so long as it is switched on, but when the stored hot water has been drawn off the flow will be reduced to almost a trickle.

The two-in-one heater

This heater is of the pressure type and is manufactured in two different sizes, 90 and 136 litres. The special feature about this type of heater is that it has twin thermostatically controlled elements, one of which, usually of 2500 watts loading, is placed in the conventional position at low level in the storage vessel whilst the other is fitted at such a level that it heats approximately 28 litres of water. Figure 20 shows a typical two-in-one heater.

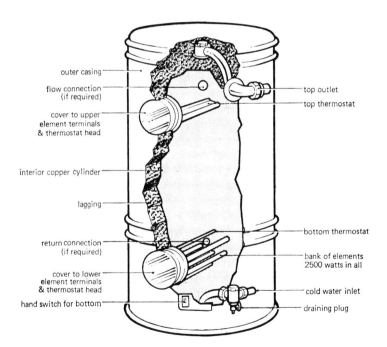

Figure 20   Two-in-one water heater

In normal operation the upper heating element is kept switched on permanently under thermostatic control while the lower element is switched on only when a larger quantity of water is required for baths or clothes washing.

This arrangement reduces the consumption of electricity in two ways. First, the heat losses from the storage vessel are reduced because of the smaller quantity of water that is kept at the storage temperature and, secondly, economy in the use of hot water is more or less enforced.

With the two-in-one heater constant hot water on tap throughout the house is provided, but the amount of hot water that is normally available at any time is limited to approximately 28 litres. This is ample for general purposes, but it will be appreciated that where the quantity is not restricted there will always be a tendency for more to be used.

Inlet baffles

All types of water heaters have some kind of device such as illustrated in Figure 21 to prevent the incoming cold water from cooling the storage unduly. The baffle usually employed is fitted at the cold-water entry so as to deflect the incoming water to the bottom of the storage vessel.

Figure 21   Inlet baffles for water heaters

Packaged plumbing unit

A self-contained unit for providing both hot and cold water for bath, basin, kitchen sink and w.c. comprises a cold-water cistern, hot-water container and pipework built into and within a rigid framework (see Figure 22).

This unit is based on a design developed by the Research and Development Group of the Ministry of Housing and Local Government, and is acceptable for the appropriate Government grants.

Figure 22   Packaged plumbing unit

It is readily handled up stairs and through doorways. It may be installed in a cupboard, against a wall, in a passage or convenient corner, or incorporated in the structure of new buildings.

The plumbing unit needs connecting only to the mains water supply, electricity supply and services as shown in the accompanying diagrams (see Figure 23A and B). There are alternative capacities available with a basic design of a 230-litre cold-water storage cistern supplying a 115- or 230-litre hot-water storage cylinder.

Figure 23   The use of a packaged plumbing unit

A *Installation with all
   services on one floor*

cold water supply
extended to
storage cistern

cold

lagging

hot

existing cold water supply
to sink or incoming cold main

electric immersion
heater and
thermostat

B *Installation servicing
   two floors and showing
   alternative connection
   with back boiler*

cold

lagging

electric immersion heater
and thermostat

back
boiler

Water heating and Economy 7

Economy 7 is a scheme providing cheap electricity between the hours of 12.30 a.m. and 7.30 a.m. It operates on one meter which has an automatic changeover from the normal unit rate to the economy rate at the prescribed time and switches back seven hours later.

There is at present a considerable difference in cost between the two unit rates, and to get the maximum benefit from Economy 7 the customer must be able to heat a substantial proportion of his water on the cheap night-time tariff.

The system should therefore be designed with sufficient storage capacity to cater for the normal needs of the maximum size of family likely to live in the dwelling. An average family uses about 136 to 159 litres of hot water daily.

It is not unusual for new homes which are to use Economy 7 to be provided with a 226-litre storage cylinder. If this supply of water is exhausted during the day some water will have to be heated at the higher daytime rate.

A number of self-contained water heaters designed specially for use with Economy 7 tariff are available.

Multiple installations

Although it is important to provide sufficient water heated on the night-time rate to cater for the main demand of the following day, it is not essential to provide all this water for the main storage vessel. As with any electrically heated water system, additional 'on the spot' heaters may be placed to avoid long 'dead legs' or difficult plumbing situations.

Two-heater cylinder

Undoubtedly, the most economical way to provide adequate hot water for a family on the Economy 7 tariff is to fit a cylinder of around 226 litres' capacity. However, there may not be sufficient space to install a cylinder of this size, and it may be necessary to limit the cylinder to a maximum of 159 litres. If the household will not generally require more than 159 litres of hot water a day, this will be quite satisfactory. If it is only necessary to heat the tank on day-time electricity to supplement the night-time charge, say once a week for the extra demand on laundry day, the average cost of electricity per unit will be near the night-time price per unit.

With only one immersion heater at the base of the storage vessel, the whole water content would be heated each time the electricity was switched on. This system would become uneconomic if the supply of hot water heated during the night ran out frequently, and day-time boosts became a regular requirement.

To ensure that only a limited amount of water is heated on the day-time rate, a second immersion heater may be fitted to the tank in a position where it will heat about 56 litres of water, before its own thermostat switches off the supply of electricity. The second immersion heater may also be manually controlled, but it will generally be more sensible for the user to leave it on all the time, since its built-in thermostat will keep it switched off until it is needed. As long as there is more than 56 litres of hot water left in the tank from the previous off-peak night-rate charge this second heater will not switch on.

It is recommended that there shall be a minimum difference of 10°C between the settings of the thermostats of the upper and lower immersion heaters. In soft-water areas the thermostat on the lower immersion heater should be set at 70°C and the thermostat on the upper immersion heater at 60°C. In hard-water areas these settings should be reduced by up to 10°C.

The minimum amount of hot water required for a bath is selected as being 56 litres – the usual last requirement of the day. The following table indicates the approximate proportions of night-time electricity, and day-time electricity used with a two-heater cylinder. The high-level element will be located to provide 56 litres of hot water in each instance. These figures are intended as a guide only, and are the result of practical trials, with the high-level heater under thermostatic control only. It will be seen from the table that even a 226-litre cylinder may sometimes need 'topping up' on day-time electricity. Since the larger cylinder could occasionally heat all of its 226 litres on day-time electricity if it were not fitted with a second heater, it could be said to be the instance where it is most important to install a second immersion heater, if there is any possibility of 226 litres being insufficient.

General Rule: Install a second immersion heater whenever possible in any cylinder if there is any possibility of the total capacity being exhausted early in the day.

Size of tank (litres)	Low level element % night units	High level element % day units
113	60	40
136	70	30
159	80	20
226	95	5

Immersion heaters for a two-heater cylinder

The upper immersion heater in a two-heater cylinder will need to keep up with demand, as far as possible, and should therefore be rated at 3 kilowatts. This will provide the fastest possible response.

The lower heater, however, has a period of approximately 7 hours in which to heat a tank full of water. In most installations, no water will be drawn off during this time, and it will only be necessary to fit a heater sufficiently large to heat the whole contents of the cylinder in, say, 6 or 7 hours. Some margin of error must be allowed for standing losses during this time.

Size of tank (litres)	Rating of low level element for Economy 7
113	1.5 kW
136	1.5 kW
159	1.5 kW
226	3.0 kW

Good installation

Because water heated at night on the Economy 7 tariff must still be hot enough for a bath in the evening, a water heating installation for this tariff must be well designed. All losses must be minimized, particularly those from mixing and single pipe circulation. The storage cylinder must be very well insulated.

6
Water Heating by Gas

The main advantages of using gas for water heating are:

1 It is clean, creates no dust or mess in the house and it conforms with the Clean Air Act. As it comes straight from a pipe it needs no storage space.
2 The hot flame of gas properly regulated heats water very fast. The instantaneous heaters provide hot water in an endless supply. The water in storage systems quickly reheats as the supply is drawn from the tank.
3 Automatic controls permit close regulation of the fuel used and allow adjustments to meet the needs of a family.
4 High efficiency of appliances reduces running costs.
5 A gas water heater may be fixed at the very point the hot water is required enabling a certain flexibility in house design and a reduction in the cost of plumbing work.

Selection of a heater

The output of a water heater is relative to the given rate of water flow and temperature rise, and although the supply of water at any required temperature is continuous, the speed of delivery is limited by the capacity of the heater. For example, although a larger heater will give hot water more quickly than a smaller one the latter will give greater efficiency and at less cost for small intermittent demands. The main consideration in selecting a heater is that it will provide the required amount of hot water to meet the demands of the family at peak times.

Instantaneous heaters

These heaters will give a continuous flow of hot water at any time within a few seconds of turning on any tap to which the heater is connected. The temperature of the water is variable according to the temperature of the cold feed, most heaters being designed to give a 26°C temperature rise. Models are available which control the water flow to give a constant outlet temperature. The flow is limited at the maximum temperature available at any time but it is usually possible to obtain a greater flow at a lower temperature without any drop in the efficiency of the heater.

Apart from the small consumption of the pilot jet, gas is used only when the water is flowing from a tap. It is the most economical form of heater and the single point type has the lowest running cost of any gas water heater. Capital and installation costs are generally less than for storage heaters giving equivalent service but the high gas rate might possibly require the fitting of larger services pipes and meters.

Since the satisfactory operation of an instantaneous heater depends on a minimum flow of water it is essential that the pressure head of the water supply is adequate. This will vary with each type of appliance and the help of the local gas regional office should be sought.

Thermostatic controls are fitted to some models ensuring that the water is supplied at a constant temperature. The correct adjustment of instantaneous heaters is more critical than that of other types and this means regular servicing is necessary to their functioning.

Some models have balanced flues which eliminate the need for a conventional chimney. Balanced-flue heaters are room sealed and must be fitted to an outside wall. The air enters and the exhaust gases pass out through the balanced flue which is completely sealed off from the room itself. The heater is therefore unaffected by room ventilation and exhaust gases cannot enter the room.

It is important to know that only balanced-flue heaters must be used for new installations in bathrooms.

Single-point heaters over a sink or washbasin must always be fitted within an arm's length (about 0.6 m) of the draw-off point. Where this is not possible the delivery may be piped to an open nozzle fixed over the sink or basin.

Instantaneous water heaters for the bathroom can be provided with an extended swivel spout to serve the bath and the washbasin provided it does not exceed 0.6 m in length. The heater must of course be fitted with a balanced flue.

Storage heaters

These units comprise a heater combined with an insulated storage vessel that will retain heated water over a period of time against a future demand. The volume of hot water they can supply is limited by the capacity, so the size of the unit must be selected carefully to meet peak demands. If it is properly sized it is unlikely that its full capacity will be used at any one time but should this occur, then the good stratification obtained with a gas storage water heater ensures that small quantities of hot water are available again within a short time. This also applies when the heater is first lit. They can be either floor standing or wall mounted and must generally be connected to a cistern supply. Some types are available with an integral feed cistern and provided these are fitted above the level of the highest draw-off tap, it will not be necessary to fit an additional feed cistern.

Sink storage heaters are available for fixing to the wall above the sink and discharge by a swivel spout of not greater than 0.6 m in length.

Gas circulators

These are in effect miniature gas boilers usually fitted near the hot-water storage cylinder. A circulator is an economical way of converting an existing water system to gas or of providing an entirely new system. Thermostatically controlled, they can also be provided with an economy valve which can be set either to heat the whole tank, or keep a few litres of water at the top of the storage cylinder constantly hot.

Gas boilers

Several types of gas boilers are available and they are ideal for a busy household needing a great deal of hot water and especially so when the prime purpose is space heating.

The modern gas boiler is a sophisticated appliance being fully automatic in action and capable of being set to follow a specific programme to the clock, making it economical to run.

The boiler indirectly heats the water in the storage cylinder whilst circulating hot water to the radiators around the house.

A modern innovation is the gas back-boiler which is an ideal replacement for the solid-fuel back-boiler. It is possible to install a very modern gas-fire and boiler with the minimum alterations to the existing pipework. The boiler is capable of providing reasonable central heating as well as hot water for domestic usage. The fire and the boiler are separately controlled and they may be used together or independently.

New design principles have enabled gas boilers to be housed in a very limited space without reducing their capacity to provide hot water. They can be wall mounted in the kitchen or anywhere else. They must of course be fixed to an outside wall.

Installation of gas appliances

The installation of gas piping and appliances must be carried out by skilled men who have a complete knowledge of the technical and safety requirements involved. They must have the proper tools and testing equipment, and the householder should know that under the Gas Safety Regulations 1972 it is in fact specified that only competent persons shall carry out gas installation work.

CORGI

The Gas Corporation in conjunction with a number of Trade Associations has set up a voluntary organization to maintain proper standards in all gas work. It is known as the Confederation for the Registration of Gas Installers and has assumed the abbreviated title of CORGI. Every plumber who contracts to do gas installation work should be registered under the scheme and householders should insist that any gas work carried out in their homes is undertaken by CORGI members only. Lists of members can be inspected at the Gas Showrooms. Every Registered CORGI gas installing business undertakes to perform gas installation and service work complying with British Standard Codes of Practice, Building Regulations and Gas Corporation requirements.

The Gas Act

Plumbers and householders should know that the Gas Act became law on 1 January 1973 and Regulations under this Act give powers to designated officers of the Gas Corporation to enter premises and cut off a supply if in the opinion of these accredited officers an installation is unsafe.

Relevant codes of practice

Reference should be made to the following Codes of Practice when installing gas supply and appliances.

COP 331 Pt. 2 1974   Installation of pipes and meters for town gas. Part 2: Metering and meter control.

COP 331 Pt. 3 1974   Installation of pipes and meters for town gas. Part 3: Installation pipes.

BS COP 5871 1980   Gas fires/boilers not exceeding 60 kw and back boilers with independent gas fire (2nd family gas).

BS COP 5376 1976   Selection and installation, gas space heating (1st and 2nd family gas).

BS COP 5546 1979   Gas supply for domestic hot-water systems (2nd family gas).

1st/2nd family gases refer to natural gases (propane, methane/North Sea).

Seven points for water heater installation

1 The site should be well-ventilated and convenient for connection to an existing flue where this is applicable. It should be noted, however, that if the appliance is to replace an existing water heater in a bathroom, only room-sealed models should be used.
2 It is preferable to keep the pipe run to the main point of usage as short as possible to minimize heat losses.
3 The existing gas installation pipes should be checked for soundness and adequacy of supply, and where applicable the flue should be checked for sufficient 'pull', correct size and suitable termination.
4 The head of water should be sufficient to operate the appliance as laid down in the manufacturer's instructions.
5 The appliance should be fixed securely, and after connection to the gas and water supplies the installation should be tested for soundness. The gas and water rates should then be adjusted to conform with the maker's instructions.
6 Check that the appliance controls are operating correctly.
7 Finally, instruct the customer on the use of the appliance, referring to the manufacturer's instructions.

Eight points for space heater installation

1 Before installation, check the chimney (flueway) for 'pull'. This can be done by holding a match near it. The flue is operating

satisfactorily if the flame is drawn into the flueway. If it burns steadily, check for restrictions in the flue; if the flame blows back, the flue is subject to down draught and may need modifications.

2 Make sure that the chimney has been swept if the fire is being sited into an open fireplace and remove or wedge fully open any damper, register plate or canopy in the fireplace opening. Make sure that there is adequate clearance at the rear and/or sides of the gas-fire flue spigot (refer to the manufacturer's instructions).

3 Check that the existing installation pipes are sound and are of adequate size.

4 When fixing the appliance a filling-in or closure plate must always be fitted. This is designed to improve the performance of the appliance. It consists usually of two openings, the top one being for the flue spigot and the lower one to provide a flue break and to assist in room ventilation. Plates are usually obtained from the appliance manufacturer or else the type is specified in the manufacturer's fixing instructions.

5 Space heaters must stand on a non-combustible material which extends 152 mm either side of the space heater and 304 mm from the back of the fireplace and is at least 15 mm thick. If the space heater is being wall mounted there should be a distance of at least 228 mm from the burner manifold and the floor level.

6 The space heater must be fitted level using the correct type of fittings and pipe as specified by the local Gas Board.

7 Test the finished installation for soundness and check the gas rate using the meter test dial and a stopwatch, and ensure that this is in accordance with the manufacturer's instructions. The gas rate can be calculated using the following formula:

$$\text{Gas rate} = \frac{\text{Heat input}}{\text{Calorific value of the gas}}$$

8 Instruct the customer on the operation of the appliance.

Five points for cooker installation

1 The siting of the appliance must be carefully considered, bearing in mind the following points:

 (a) It should be in a well-ventilated position.

 (b) There should be sufficient natural light to ensure that it can be used with safety.

(c) There should be sufficient clearance to ensure that it can be used without obstruction, in other words there should be room to open the oven door.

(d) It should be in a convenient position for use by the customer, i.e. near to preparation space.

2 Follow the maker's instructions carefully when assembling the appliance. Check that the existing installation pipes are sound and are of adequate size.

3 When connecting the appliance use only recommended fittings, ensuring that there is a means of disconnection. The appliance must be fitted level – this is important for all appliances but particularly in the case of cookers where pans of liquid will be placed on them.

4 When the appliance has been connected again test the installation for soundness. Check that the appliance controls are functioning correctly and test any concealed supplies on the appliance for soundness, i.e. the grill and oven supplies.

5 Before leaving the premises ensure that pilots have been relit and above all explain the operation of the appliance in detail to the customer. Suggest that the customer operates the appliance after instruction to ensure that he or she has understood the explanation; and give the customer the manufacturer's customer instruction leaflet for future reference. It is advisable not to leave the fitting instruction with the customer as this may tempt do-it-yourself enthusiasts to attempt any servicing or repair work.

Gas supply

The gas meter should be capable of passing the full consumption of the heater in addition to the requirements of all other appliances, and it is preferable to run in an independent supply from the meter to the heater. If this is not possible it will be advisable to ensure that the heater receives the first delivery of gas from the meter, and that the pipe sizes are adequate to give a full gas supply irrespective of demands. Gas supply pipes which run between joists under floor-boards should be in hard metal and not in copper tube or plastic pipes, which could easily be penetrated by a nail.

A full-bore gas cock should be fitted close to appliances to facilitate maintenance without interrupting the gas supply to other parts of the house.

Cold-water supply

To ensure a constant pressure and flow of water to a water heater it should be fed by a single pipe from the storage cistern of the house. In certain circumstances mains water supply may be used but it is always advisable to consult the local water undertaking on this point.

The most important considerations are to see to it that:

(a) Pipe sizes are adequate to pass the required water flow at the prevailing pressure.
(b) Pipe runs are as short as possible.
(c) A fixed jumper stopcock of an approved pattern is fitted on the cold-water inlet as close as possible to the heater to isolate it when repairs are necessary.

Hot-water draw-off

The pipe run should be as short as possible to avoid heat loss and waste of water. The most used draw-off point should have the shortest run. In no case should the maximum pipe run exceed 8 m.

Single point heaters have open outlet spouts and on no account should any additional fittings or other obstruction be connected to the outlet side of the heater. Any such connection would result in damage to the heating body.

Ventilation

The ventilation requirements for heater compartments and various types of rooms are under constant review by technical committees concerned with gas installation. As knowledge of this complex subject increases, amendments to the regulations are made. It is advisable for the installer to keep himself up-to-date with the regulations issued from the Gas Corporation Research and Development Department.

Flues

The installer is very much concerned with flues and should have a sound knowledge of their basic principles because of the safety factors involved.

In any fuel burning appliance the hot products of combustion, being less dense than air, will have a tendency to flow upwards in a flue or chimney. With a modern high-efficiency gas water heater, so much heat is removed from the product of combustion that it is of the utmost importance to plan the flue in such a way to conserve fully the residual heat of the product and to ensure that no resistance is offered to the free flow of flue gases. A permanent state of down-draught can be set up which the heater may be unable to overcome due to the excessive cooling of the flue gases – for example, in a long length of flue exposed outside a building.

The flue terminal

The flue terminal should offer the minimum resistance to combustion products and have a free area equal at least to twice the nominal area of the flue.

There should be outlets on opposite, or all sides except where the design is such as to provide extraction under all wind conditions.

It should have effective protection against entry of birds, leaves, rain or snow, and the minimum dimension of any opening should be not less than 6.35 mm or greater than 14.3 mm.

Construction of the flue

The material of the flue must be resistant to temperatures up to 95°C. It must have low conductivity and be resistant to acids. This precludes the use of untreated metal flues.

The flue must be run as far as possible under cover to minimize cooling.

The flue must be of the specified size and there must be no reduction in the cross-sectional area at any point. The ideal shape is circular and this should be adhered to as far as is practical.

The interior surface of the flue must be smooth and free from projections, and there should be a rising tendency along its entire length and sharp changes of direction avoided. The horizontal length of the flue should not exceed 1.20 m.

If the flue is of excessive length or if for any reason the flue gases are likely to become cooled below the dewpoint, provision must be made for disposal of the condensate.

Excessive dilution of the products of combustion with cool air should be avoided and this precludes the use of common flues, open tees or any form of extra air inlet.

In the case of persistent down-draught or where static conditions are encountered, the flue installation must be re-designed to conform to the foregoing principles.

Balanced flues

The development of the balanced flue has enabled the fixing of water heaters in positions not suitable for the more conventional type of appliance. The balanced-flue heater does not need a draught diverter nor any additional flue equipment inside the room. It therefore presents a neat appearance and is more easily fitted where headroom is limited.

Balanced-flue terminals should not be fitted in any position which would allow combustion products to feed back through adjacent doors or windows. These positions include, immediately beneath eaves or a balcony, at a re-entrant position on the face of the building, or adjacent to any projection on the face of the building.

Other advantages are:

(a) They can be installed in positions not suitable for conventional water heaters.
(b) The terminal is fairly inconspicuous, and a vertical flue pipe is not required. This is particularly important in new housing and has been welcomed by architects.

Water heaters as auxiliaries

A multi-point heater may be connected to a boiler system as an alternative and continuous source of hot-water supply during the summer months, and is similarly available for immediate use whenever the boiler is inoperative. The combined installation of heater and boiler is simple as the same hot-water draw-off piping may be used for both units, the isolation of one system from the other being effected by the operation of one or more stopcocks or a two-way valve. The heater is not, however, suitable for operation as a booster and must therefore be supplied with cold water. Whichever cold- and hot-water systems of supply are adopted the expansion pipe must always remain open to the atmosphere, and to the hot-water storage tank when the boiler is in use, but must be capable of isolation from the heater when the latter is in operation. An isolating stopcock ('B' in Figure 24) must therefore be incorporated and a second stopcock ('A' in Figure 24) is required to turn off the supply to the heater when the boiler is in use.

When it is proposed to fit a gas water heater as an alternative to a solid-fuel heating system, a careful study of the existing plumbing should be made and the layout sketched accurately after all the pipes have been traced and their purpose determined.

Figure 24   Water heater as an auxiliary

cold water ———— - - - - - - ╮ additional for 'Ascot'
hot water ▬▬▬ ▬ ▬ ▬ ▬ ▬ ▬ ╯

Water supply

The cold-water supply to the heater should be taken from the cold-water storage cistern in one of the following ways.

1 By means of an independent supply pipe direct from the cistern to the heater.
2 By teeing from the cold down service between the supply cistern and the cold-water taps in the bathroom.
3 By teeing off from the existing cold-water supply pipe to the hot water tank, but at a point above the level of the top of this tank.

Where there is insufficient height from cistern supply, the heater may be connected direct to the incoming cold main provided the following conditions are observed.

(a) That permission of the Local Water Authority is obtained.
(b) That no connection is made between the outlet of the heater and any pipe connected to any tank. This necessitates the fitting of independent taps for the heater delivery.

Whichever system is employed, the existing expansion pipe must always remain open to atmosphere and to the hot tank or cylinder, but the draw-off pipe must be capable of isolation from the expansion pipe and from the whole boiler system.

The correct procedure for the change-over from one system to the other should be fully understood by the consumer, otherwise an incorrect sequence may be carried out, resulting in unsatisfactory operation of the heater when, for example, both stopcocks are left open.

Simple boiler system for the supply of domestic hot water

The incorporation of a multi-point heater to operate as an alternative to the existing system can be arranged by following the lay-out shown in Figure 24 provided the hot-water feed pipe from the boiler to the kitchen sink is 22-mm nominal bore.

1 The heater is supplied direct with cold water via a 22-mm distributing pipe from the cold-water supply tank.
2 A stopcock 'A' of approved pattern is fitted to this pipe close to the inlet of the heater.
3 The outlet of the heater is connected by a short length of 22-mm pipe to the 22-mm draw-off pipe from the boiler system, but close to the sink tap.
4 A second cock 'B' is fitted to the boiler system draw-off pipe between the expansion pipe and the first branch, thus isolating all hot draw-off pipes from the boiler system when the heater is put into operation.

To change from Boiler to Heater:

1 Close stopcock 'B'
2 Open stopcock 'A'

To change from Heater to Boiler:

1 Close stopcock 'A'
2 Open stopcock 'B'

Alternatively the heater may be connected by adopting the following methods:

1 The 22-mm cold-water supply is taken from the cold feed to the hot cylinder at a point above the level of the top of the hot-water tank.
2 A stopcock 'A' of approved design is fitted close to the inlet of the heater.

The following alternative hot-water draw-off should be utilized where the hot-water feed pipe to the kitchen sink is 15-mm nominal bore.

1 A separate 22-mm pipe is run from the outlet of the heater to a second hot-water tap at the sink.
2 From this point a 22-mm hot-water pipe is run to a two-way cock situated on the hot-water draw-off pipe between the hot-water tank and the nearest draw-off branch. Care must be taken to see that the two-way cock is fitted in such a way as to give the correct alternative paths.

Metric units for gas

	Imperial unit	Metric unit
1. Pressure	inches water gauge (in.wg)	millibar (mbar)
	pounds per square inch (p.s.i.)	bar (bar)
2. Standard reference conditions for gas volumes		
Temperature	60° Fahrenheit (60°F)	15° Celsius (15°C)
Pressure	30 inches of mercury (30″Hg)	1013.25 mbar
Condition	saturated with water	dry
3. Sales unit	Therm	One hundred megajoules (100 MJ)

4. *Calorific value*	British Thermal Units per cubic foot (Btu/cu.ft)	megajoules per cubic metre (MJ/m³)
5. *Heat rate*	British Thermal Units per hour (Btu/hr)	kilowatt (kW) OR, where information may be required to calculate running costs, megajoules per hour will be given *in addition to* kilowatts – e.g. kW(MJ/h)

7

Domestic Central Heating

The requirements of human beings vary considerably when it comes to personal comforts and they are influenced by age, sex, state of health, personal preferences and prejudices. The heating engineer must be guided by his customer in deciding the temperatures for the various parts of the house in which he is installing a central heating plant.

However, there are general guidelines and it is accepted by the heating trade that 21°C is a suitable temperature for the living room, 13 to 16°C for bedrooms, 16 to 18°C for bathroom and 16°C for most other areas of the house.

In trying to achieve comfort conditions to his customer's requirements, the heating engineer will take into account the type of house construction, its situation, local climatic conditions, the state of doors, windows and the roof within the house, because all these factors affect his recommendations in the matters of heating form and the appliances to be installed.

The engineer will make a careful survey of the house and from his findings and measurements he will make elaborate calculations. In these calculations he is mainly concerned with heat losses. In this matter, the wise householder will concern himself with insulation before he decides on the installation of any form of central heating. The golden rule is to keep the cold out of the house rather than warm it continuously once it has penetrated the holes, openings, cracks and surfaces. Half the cost of heating in most houses arises from poor or below standard insulation. Anyone who has installed a good double glazing system will understand this all-important point.

The reputable heating engineer will be prepared to advise the householder, and from the results of his survey be able to discuss the best methods of heating the house. He will make recommendations on (1) full-house heating by which every part of the house will be heated constantly to a specified temperature, (2) part-house heating which, as the term implies, will give specific temperatures to selected rooms or parts of the house and (3) background heating by which the whole or part of the house is heated and the temperature maintained at a lower level, supplemented by local heat for bodily comfort.

There is a wide variety of choice today from which to select the type of heating installation to suit individual needs. There can be no 'cheap' installation and householders are advised to seek only the services of qualified installers. Beware of the door-to-door salesman and the man who wishes to work in the evening or at the weekend. People have suffered a great deal from the unqualified charlatans who call themselves plumbers and heating engineers without any right to the titles.

Small pipe central heating

In this chapter we concern ourselves with those forms of heating commonly known as 'smallbore' and 'microbore' (also known as 'minibore').

It is not possible in this book to cover the subject in detail because central heating in any form is a specialized subject and serious study is required if any plumber is intending to set himself up as an installer. The following is intended as a guide only and would-be designers and installers should read and digest the valuable technical literature obtainable from the British Standards Institution, Institution of Heating and Ventilating Engineers, Institute of Plumbing, British Gas Corporation, Electricity Council, Copper Development Association and others.

The original purpose of developing the smallbore heating system was to heat a dwelling of up to 140-m² floor area. It is nevertheless possible to install the system in premises having a much larger area, provided the installation can be designed round a centrally placed heating unit, making it possible to design the piping layout to include more but shorter pipe circuits.

Briefly, the smallbore heating system comprises a boiler to which radiators are connected by means of small diameter tubes, and heated water being forced through the tubes and radiators by means of a specially designed pump or circulator.

To ensure proper temperature control, an automatically operated mixing valve is used in conjunction with a by-pass pipe. This
mixing valve, which is actuated by the outside air temperature, thus
ensures that the heat output from the radiators is controlled under
such weather conditions, without affecting the boiler temperature.
Such an arrangement ensures that adequate heat is available in the
boiler to give an abundant and constant supply of domestic hot
water.

Domestic hot-water supply

On the domestic hot water side, it is essential to use an indirect
copper cylinder coupled to the boiler by an independent gravity
circuit. This circuit is normally run in 22-mm or 28-mm copper
tubing and is entirely separate from the radiator runs, apart from
the permissible case of a towel rail being fitted.

The purpose of using an indirect cylinder is that it will act as an
accumulator to absorb any excess heat in the boiler, in the event of a
sudden reduction in the required heating load and until the boiler
damper control in a solid-fuel system slows down the burning rate.

Returning to the heating side of the installation, it is generally
only necessary to use 15-mm-diameter copper tubes in the heating
circuits apart from where the circuits run into a common flow and
return. At such points these common mains would be increased to
22 mm.

The use of small-diameter copper tubes in the heating mains
means that there is no need to hide them from view, as they are neat
in appearance and can be run so as to blend with the surroundings.
The pump allows great freedom in deciding pipe runs, thus permitting easy installation without costly structural work or damage to
interior decorations. Furthermore, a considerable saving in pipe
length is achieved because it is not necessary to rise above the floor
levels on which the radiators are to be fitted; this, in turn, results in
lower heat losses from the distribution system and a consequent
saving in fuel.

There are now on the market materials other than copper tube
which are eminently suitable not only for smallbore central heating
but for all water service pipes, both hot and cold. The most notable
of these is probably CPVC – notable because it is a plastic which,
until recent times, was considered unsuitable for hot water.

CPVC (chlorinated polyvinyl chloride) systems have been exten-
sively used in America since 1965, where the Genova Company led

the way. With this background of experience, Hunter Building Products Ltd, in England, began the manufacture of Hunter Genova CPVC at their London factory in 1979. The material has an Agrément Certificate and a British Standard is expected to be published in the near future.

The inertness of CPVC, coupled with the smooth bore of the pipe and fittings, almost completely eliminates scale build-up within piping systems. Because CPVC is not a conductor of electricity, problems of galvanic corrosion do not occur and the piping system will never suffer from oxidative corrosion. CPVC is *not* recommended for use as gas pipes.

High standards of quality control are enforced in the manufacture of these products and in addition piping assemblies are regularly submitted to hydrostatic and thermocycling test procedures. In these, pipe and fittings must be able to withstand a sustained hydrostatic pressure of 12 bar (172 p.s.i.) for 10,000 hours (416 days) at a temperature of 82°C without leakage; and pipe and fittings are subjected to a pressure of 7 bar (103 p.s.i.) with the temperature of the water alternating between 82°C and 15°C for 10,000 cycles, taking a total of 55 days.

Hunter Genova pipe is available in 15, 22 and 28 mm sizes and a full range of fittings enables connections to be made easily to other materials, such as copper and iron pipes. CPVC pipe is joined to fittings by solvent welding, a simple technique which gives a bond almost stronger than the pipe itself.

Tests by independent laboratories have shown that the CPVC material and the Nova Weld C solvent cement used in the Hunter Genova system pass all the National Water Council requirements for toxicity, taste, and resistance to microbiological growth.

CPVC, like all organic materials, will burn in a conflagration. However, its flash ignition temperature is some 110°C better than normal uPVC, a material that has wide acceptance in the building industry.

Systems are designed in the normal way, with the following points in mind. Never connect CPVC directly to a boiler or other heat-generating source. Come away from the boiler with a 380-mm (or more) length of copper pipe to allow the intense heat to dissipate. Similarly, do not let CPVC come close to articles which are likely to become very hot.

CPVC is not a conductor of electricity and so cannot be used for earthing.

CPVC is a pliable material with good insulating properties (water in Genova tube takes four times as long to freeze as water in copper pipes), but even so, care must be taken to protect it by lagging all external pipework or where pipework may be affected by frost.

In general, the strength of CPVC pipe is more than adequate to withstand treatment likely to be encountered in normal installations. However, it is not recommended that attempts be made to bend CPVC pipe substantially, and all changes in direction must therefore be made by using the appropriate fittings. This is easily done with Nova Weld C solvent cement and the appropriate Hunter Genova fittings. Solvent cementing should not be attempted in wet conditions or at temperatures below 0°C or above 40°C.

Figure 25   How to plumb an expansion tank with Hunter Genova fittings

The pipe runs need not be laid with a constant rise or fall for ventilating purposes. Inverted loop circuits, such as may be met in running round the door casings, may be used, without fear of air-locking the system. Air-cocks fitted at such points are used only during the initial filling up of the installation. Generally, single pipe circuits connecting two or more radiators are used, the temperature difference between the flow and return being of the order of 11°C. With such a low differential the radiators are all maintained at more or less the same temperature. Obviously, the number of circuits used in any given installation will vary according to the type of dwelling involved, the positioning of the rooms and whether it is a house or bungalow. In general, the normal house would have two, or at the most three, major pipe circuits with perhaps a short loop feeding a single radiator as might be required in a hall or cloakroom.

To ensure that the full benefit of a smallbore heating system is obtained, it is advisable to insulate the roof space so as to avoid loss of heat and consequent waste of fuel. The domestic hot-water storage cylinder should be fitted with an insulating jacket and where, as in the case of a bungalow, any pipes are run in the roof space, they must be protected against heat loss.

Design

In designing a smallbore heating installation the following procedure should be adopted:

1 Decide the required room temperature and then calculate the heat losses through walls, floors, ceilings, etc.
2 Plan radiator positions and pipe runs.
3 Calculate the friction losses in pipe circuits, and determine from these the pump size.
4 Size the radiators and boiler.

Room temperature requirements may vary from client to client, but generally the room temperatures recommended in British Standard Code of Practice CP 3006, Part 1: 1969 will find ready acceptance. Thus the following temperatures can be taken as giving comfort conditions:

21°C for living-rooms.
13°C for bedrooms.
16°C for hall and staircase.

Where a room is used only intermittently and for comparatively short periods, such as a dining-room, it is advisable to adopt a design temperature of 21°C, thus ensuring a quicker warming-up of the room concerned. Generally with ordinary domestic premises there is sufficient heat available in the kitchen from the boiler itself and the various hot-water pipe mains and flue pipes to maintain an adequate temperature. Where an outside boiler is used provision must be made to warm the kitchen and in this case 18°C will be found to be a satisfactory temperature.

The foregoing temperatures are those required to give full central heating comfort. Where, however, open fires are to be used with the smallbore heating system providing only background heating, 16°C may be taken as the design temperature for living-rooms. With the room temperatures decided, the heat requirements can now be calculated, starting off by taking the difference between outside and selected inside temperatures to give the temperature difference rise, the outside temperature always being taken as 1°C.

The heat loss through walls, ceilings, floors and windows is then dealt with. The amount of heat lost through these surfaces is known as thermal transmission, which in turn can be defined as the amount of heat in watts (W) which will flow through 1 m² of a particular type and thickness of construction when the temperatures of the air adjoining the inner and outer faces differ by 1°C. This is called the 'U value' and for the convenience of the heating designer complete tables giving the U values for most forms of construction are available in table form from the British Standards Institution and the Institution of Heating and Ventilating Engineers.

The formula for calculating heat transmission through a structure is $H = U(ti - to) \times A$, where H is the heat transmission, U the transmission coefficient of the structure, W/m²/°C, ti is the inside air temperature, to is the outside air temperature and A is the area of the structure.

Air changes must be allowed for when calculating heat losses and this applies particularly to rooms with large open fireplaces, which will withdraw air at least three times that necessary for normal ventilation purposes. In houses having central heating it will be found that the room temperature will drop several degrees when an open fire is lit. The use of a modern fireplace with an adjustable restrictive flue throat can keep the flow of air to chimney to a minimum in such circumstances.

In the case of 'open plan' types of houses it is generally necessary to assume a room temperature of 21°C and maintain this for calculation purposes throughout the whole house.

Having completed the calculations for each room they are added together to give the total heat losses throughout the house. The total is defined in watts.

The next step is to plan the radiator positions and pipe runs. This is a matter that requires some care. Wherever possible, radiators should be sited under windows. The advantages gained thereby are as follows:

They make use of areas not normally occupied.
They avoid the soiling of decorations by dust-laden convection currents.
They overcome down-draught.
They provide better temperature distribution through the room.

In some cases, particularly in existing premises, built-in furniture may make siting of radiators under a window impossible, and they may have to be mounted on or against a full wall. Under these conditions, one should always fit a canopy across the full length of the radiator top to prevent staining of the walls and ceilings by dust-laden convection currents.

In preparing a plan of the pipe runs, it should always be borne in mind that the shorter the pipe circuit the better. The plan itself should be drawn to a sufficiently large scale for all pipe runs, with the positions of valves clearly indicated. Later as each pipe circuit is sized, the pipe diameter should be marked on the drawing. If an isometric projection is drawn, quantities may be read off from it.

Friction losses

With the pipe circuit, radiators and valves marked on the drawing, the next step is to calculate the friction losses through the pipe runs, to ensure that they come within the pressure head range of the available and suitable types of pumps. It is here that the choice of copper tube, as a suitable material to use, becomes a major factor. The smooth internal surface, allied to a slightly larger bore than the equivalent iron tube, gives a much lower friction factor. Further, as the manufacturing tolerances for copper tubes are much less than is the case with iron pipes, greater accuracy is obtained in calculating friction losses. Added to this, the copper tube has a slightly smaller outside diameter, making for neater appearance.

To arrive at the friction losses in the pipe circuits, these are each measured separately to give the actual length of pipe in each circuit, to which is added an allowance of one-third to cover the frictional resistance of fittings and valves, etc. While this may seem an arbitrary method to adopt it is indeed one that has been found to give very satisfactory results.

Heating load

The heating load will be taken by the radiators and it will be equal to the total heat losses, less the heat emitted from exposed pipework in the various rooms. Tables are available to enable calculations to be made of the heat emission from runs of pipe of differing diameters but broadly speaking, emission from pipe and radiator surfaces depends on the difference between the mean temperature of the water in the system, and the room temperature. In forced circulation systems the temperature drop will be between 11°C and 16°C and this differential affects pipe sizing insofar as it determines the rate of water circulation and, consequently, the frictional resistance of the circuit.

By adopting the higher differential of 16°C the water circulation will be lowered thereby reducing friction. On the other hand, this differential means a lower difference between the water temperature in the system and the room temperature, and this could call for larger radiators in certain rooms and the possible need of 22-mm connections. For this reason the 11°C is generally adopted for smallbore systems. This lower differential ensures that the radiators at the extreme ends of the circuit will receive water at higher temperatures, and also allows a rapid heating up of the system from cold.

Frictional resistance is an important factor in pumped circulations and in the event of the resistance of a circuit being greater than the available circulating head, the circuit must be re-designed to give a smaller total length. Alternatively, the designer can regroup the radiators to give an additional circuit, thus spreading the heating load. As already mentioned it might be advisable to increase the pipe size to 22 mm for part of the main circuit. On the other hand, the higher differential of 16°C might solve the problem because the effect of this would be to lessen the frictional resistance in the main circuit.

Where two or more circuits share common flow and return mains, the heating loads of the circuits served must be calculated and used to obtain the resistance of the common mains from the graph. Equally, the heating load of the common mains, by emission and any radiators they feed, must be divided proportionately between the circuits they serve.

The short connecting mains between the various radiator circuits and boiler are usually 22-mm tubes, except where there are four or more separate radiator circuits; in these cases, a 28-mm diameter tube should be used.

Size of radiators

Finally, it is necessary to calculate the radiator surface area that each room requires and to choose the type most suitable for the purpose. To calculate the radiator surface for any room, first take the actual metre run of exposed pipe in that room and multiply this length by the emission factor. This figure is then subtracted from the total heat requirement of the room, which had previously been found. The remainder is divided by the radiator transmission factor for an average temperature difference between the water in the radiator and the ambient air, to give the total radiator surface required.

With the normal steel radiators, an average transmission factor of 23.8 W/m/°C may be accepted. Working with this factor and knowing the length of exposed pipe in the room, the required radiator area for a room with a heat loss of 2.344 kW and having 6.09 m run of exposed pipe, 3.8 m² of radiator surface would suffice.

Generally, the choice of the particular type of radiator used is a matter for consultation with the householder. Panel wall radiators are very popular if there is enough space available to accommodate the required length.

Size of boiler

There is now only the boiler to consider. Whether it be gas-fired, oil or solid-fuel burning depends on the householder's preference but it must be capable of meeting the maximum demand likely to be imposed by the heating system, plus an adequate margin to cover the needs of the domestic hot-water supply. A minimum of 3.517 kW should be allowed for this latter, over and above the total central heating needs. The boiler must be fitted with a thermostat that is reliable in action, to ensure good control of the burning rate. It is recommended that the boiler manufacturer be consulted regarding any particular appliances.

Since the introduction of smallbore heating, a number of boiler manufacturers have devoted considerable attention to reducing the running costs of heating systems. The result is that today there are excellent clock-controlled boilers that are designed to operate separate circuits for day or night only as required. This is achieved by having two separate flow connections, one running to the bedrooms or night areas, and the other to the living rooms or day areas. By pre-setting the separate clocks on each of these circuits they are automatically switched on or off, thus providing heat in the required places at the appropriate times. The result is that with such installations a much smaller boiler is used and it therefore operates at a constant and high efficiency. As a case in point, where under ordinary conditions a boiler of 13.19 kW would be necessary, a clock-controlled boiler of 9.68 kW only would be called for.

Pump and control equipment

Smallbore copper tube forced circulating heating systems can only work if the correct type of pump is used. There are a number of suitable makes available, and all of these are of the 'canned rotor' type, without glands between the motor and the impeller. The advantages of this form of construction are: (1) no possibility of water leaking out, and (2) as the bearings are water lubricated, no periodical oiling or greasing is necessary. The electric motor itself is of the squirrel cage induction type, powering a 3-speed pump with a wattage consumption depending on pump speed as follows: speed 1, 40 watts; speed 2, 65 watts; speed 3, 105 watts.

Grundfos Pumps market two models for domestic installations: the Standard Selectric Mark 2 UPS 15-50, suitable for the average house smallbore system; and the Super Selectric High Head UPS 18-60, for large boiler and high-resistance systems (low water content, microbore and automatic-valve radiators). The pumps work under a maximum pressure of 10 bar (147 p.s.i.).

Also available with these pumps are fittings to provide connection to iron or copper pipes, and isolating valves and reducers.

The motor and impeller are, to all intents and purposes, silent in operation, which is important when the pump may be required to run at night, though care should be taken in installation to avoid transmitted noise through pipework, which can be a constant source of annoyance.

Circulator

The circulator should, whenever possible, be installed in the return main. The reason for this is that it is then operating at a lower temperature than would be the case if it were fitted into the flow pipe and can, if need be, have cork blocks mounted underneath as a stand and to prevent vibration. With installations having heating mains at a level below that of the expansion tank which is less than the pressure head developed by the circulator, it should be fitted in the flow-pipe to avoid the likelihood of sub-atmospheric pressures in the high-level mains. Such conditions may sometimes be encountered in fitting heating installations in bungalows, where the pipe circuits may be run at or near ceiling level.

It is important to note that, because of the close fit between the impeller and the case, all parts of the installation should be thoroughly cleaned and flushed out to remove any swarf or other foreign matter likely to jam the pump or cause damage to the bearings.

Electrical starting gear

In dealing with the electrical starting gear, it is imperative that the push-button starter recommended and supplied by the pump manufacturers should be used. This is fitted with the correct current overload release to protect the field coils of the motor from possible damage by over-heating or burning out in the event of the impeller becoming jammed.

Control equipment

With a smallbore heating system using only a small amount of water working under forced circulation, a very large degree of flexibility is available. Because of this, individual radiators may be turned on or off to suit any given requirements. With the small amount of water used, and that under pressure, there is no long waiting period between turning on any radiator and that radiator reaching the correct operating temperature. However, it is desirable that some method of controlling the entire system in relation to the outside air temperatures should be fitted to every smallbore heating installation. Such form of control will ensure economic running of the system and at the same time provide a constant and adequate supply of domestic hot water. It may be thought that control by the boiler thermostat alone would be a satisfactory method to adopt. It cannot be emphasized too strongly that such a practice must be avoided, because if such control were used, the closing down of the boiler firing rate would equally cut the heat output to the domestic water side.

Control methods

The ideal method of control is one that is fully automatic and works through a temperature-sensitive bulb fitted outside the house. A capillary tube runs from the bulb to a three-way control valve fitted to the flow-pipe from the boiler and a by-pass connecting it to the main return pipe. The temperature-sensitive element, being continuously in operation, opens or closes the mixing valve on the heating mains conversely with the outside temperature and thus maintains, within limits, the room temperature at a constant figure. The motive power to operate the control comes from the pressure differential across the pump. By using this type of control unit, all rooms are maintained at the correct temperature and localized air disturbances caused by open doors and windows in some rooms do not affect other rooms. The small additional cost of this piece of equipment should, it is claimed, be recouped over two or three heating seasons by reason of the expected saving in fuel costs.

An alternative method of control is to use room thermostats coupled to the pump, thereby controlling the amount of heat passed to the radiators. There are, however, a number of disadvantages attached to this , such as finding suitable positions for mounting and the cost of installing the necessary switch and electric mains wiring. Similarly, individual radiator thermostatic control would be expensive and would leave the heating mains 'alive' with a consequent waste of fuel.

The only other way of dealing with the problem is to install a three-way by-pass valve connected between flow and return mains, and to adjust the valve manually. This entails the householder altering the setting to meet outside temperature variations.

A variation of the three-way by-pass valve is also available. It consists of an automatic three-way mixing valve, with a bimetal spiral in the upper part of the valve casing, controlling the movement of the double clack in the lower part, which either opens the inlet port or closes the return port, so that a mixed flow temperature can be selected and maintained.

Isolating valves

It is advisable to provide an isolating valve on both the flow and return mains. This will allow the radiators and pipe circuits to be drained without shutting down the boiler and domestic hot-water supply side of the system. The valve on the flow main only may be closed in the event of wishing to shut down the central heating circuits. If the valve on the return were closed, there would be a likelihood of high pressure occurring in the heating system due to the expansion of water.

Lockshield valves should be mounted on the return main of all secondary circuits; this will enable the circulation to be reduced to the required rate and will also prevent 'short-circuiting' of the major circuits. The adjustment of the lockshield valves on the secondary circuits is carried out when the system is first put into use, so that with all the radiators working, the water in the return mains from all circuits is at the same temperature.

Installation

The technique of installing smallbore copper tubes is a matter with which plumbers and heating engineers are familiar as part of their normal work. Copper tubing used for a heating installation is dealt with in the same way. It must, however, be realized that with a smallbore heating installation, most of the pipes are run on wall surfaces and are plainly visible. Under such conditions, the instal-ling of pipe runs and fittings must be done in the neatest manner, so that the completed job is unobtrusive and harmonizes with the surrounding decorations. In a new house, it is preferable that the pipework should be done after plastering has been finished, but prior to the completion of the painting and decorating.

It is because of this need for neatness that light gauge copper tubes are so suitable. Copper pipes do not rust and painting is unnecessary. In addition, the ductility of the metal allows it to be manipulated with ease, whilst the strength of light gauge copper tube is more than adequate for the service it has to perform.

The smooth internal surfaces are important because of the low frictional resistance they offer to the flow of water.

From the decorative point of view, the smooth non-rusting exter-nal surfaces have much to commend them; they can be polished easily and readily take a plated finish, features that can be exploited to fit in with the surrounding decorative treatment.

Joints

The jointing of the copper tubes may be carried out with either capillary soldered fittings or compression fittings.

In general, the type of joint chosen must not in any way restrict the bore of the tube, and in addition should preferably be so fixed to allow for easy dismantling. This last point is of particular importance where it may be necessary to provide additional circuits or radiators at a later date. It has been found that many people, when having central heating installed, try to save money by cutting down the number of radiators initially installed. In such cases, provision for the additional circuits can always be made by inserting tee-pieces at the required points and blanking off the branches.

Clips

The stand-off type of clip should always be used and spaced at intervals of not more than 1.25 m. This type of clip holds the pipe off the wall approximately 0.10 mm and thereby prevents possible damage to paintwork through overheating. It allows easy cleaning of the pipes and gives sufficient room for painting the surface behind them.

Where inverted pipe loops are formed in passing over doorways and similar obstructions, experience has shown that it is not necessary to fit open vents at these points. Ventcocks should be fitted on any loop or circuit that cannot be cleared of air through the radiators, for use when first filling up the system. In the same way, draincocks should be fitted in the return main near to the boiler and also on any circuit run at a level below that of the boiler.

Expansion cistern

As with every other hot-water heating system, a separate expansion cistern must be fitted from which cold-water feed is taken and connected into the return main close to the boiler. The cold-water feed-pipe should be connected to the bottom of the heating return main by means of a 'U' bend, or taken in at the side. The by-pass connections should be made with swept tees. Expansion pipes should not be smaller than 22 mm diameter.

Types of radiators

The type of radiator is a matter of individual preference. Consistent with its having the required heating surface, one or other of the many types of the wall, free standing, skirting panel or floorline patterns can be used.

Wall radiators should be mounted above the skirting and have at least 127 mm between the centre line of the bottom tappings and the heating main. It must be remembered that if the radiator is fixed too high on the wall, a higher temperature gradient between floor and ceiling will occur. Connections to radiators may be made either to the bottom tappings or to one top and one bottom tapping. A wheel-head valve should be fitted to the flow connection and a loose key, lockshield valve to the return connection on each radiator. Balancing of water flow through the radiators is achieved by adjusting the lockshield valve, while the wheel-head valve is used to turn the radiator on and off.

In designing an installation, the use of radiators with heat emission greater than 2.05 kW should, if possible, be avoided. Two small radiators to give the required heating surface would be better, otherwise with a large radiator the connections may have to be increased in size to 22 mm.

Skirting heating panels

If it is desired to use skirting heating panels, care must be taken to see that the connections are fitted in such a way that by turning off the heat it does not interfere with the flow of hot water to heating units in other rooms. Heat emission data for skirting heating, convector heaters or similar units must be obtained from the manufacturers.

Where a pipe has to pass through a wall or ceiling a 28-mm copper or brass sleeve should be fitted after drilling the hole in the required position. Powered angle drills are available which enable clean neat holes to be drilled close in to the corner.

Connections to the boiler

In connecting the return main to the boiler, it is essential that the stream of water returning under pressure is not injected into the return pipe of the domestic hot-water system. This could give rise to reverse circulation to the indirect cylinder. If there is only one return tapping on the boiler, a twin elbow or pitcher tee should be used and the lead to the heating main reduced to the required pipe size. Where it is more convenient to take both the heating and domestic flow mains from a single boiler tapping, a 35-mm pitcher tee with a reduced branch should be used to ensure an adequate supply to the gravity circulating primary side of the hot-water storage cylinder.

Thermometers

Thermometers should be fitted, one on the boiler and a second in the flow-pipe past the by-pass and control valve. The latter will give the temperature of the water going to the radiators as distinct from the boiler water.

Flushing

Finally, before the completed installation is put into service the whole system, boiler, pipework, cistern and radiators, must be thoroughly flushed out at least three times to ensure removal of swarf, filings and any dirt that may be present. This is a most important factor in ensuring a fully successful and trouble-free heating system. In this connection it must be remembered how necessary it is to remove cutting burrs when the tube has been cut to the required lengths.

If, as in the case of cast-iron radiators, it is necessary to paint them, it should be remembered that metallic paints reduce the heat transmission by approximately 15 per cent. With ordinary paints or enamels the efficiency is not affected.

Micro and Minibore heating

Following development work during the late 1960s the Wednesbury Tube Company introduced their 'Microbore' system in 1968. The Copper Development Association had published details of the system known as 'Minibore' in 1967 and many hundreds of these systems were installed and those in service are said to have fully justified the claims made in the early stages, proving them to be efficient and economical both in materials and labour.

The basic principles of microbore and minibore heating follow closely those of a standard smallbore heating system. In fact, the principles and practices laid down in the Standard Code of Practice for smallbore central heating installation should be followed.

There are two basic systems of this development in small pipe heating: (1) open tank (see Figure 26A) and (2) sealed tank (Figure 26B).

The low-pressure system is the most frequently installed of the two, although the pressurized system is becoming recognized now because of the higher temperatures that can be achieved using smaller heating units. Both systems employ 8-mm or 10-mm tubes on the radiator circuits and these are connected to flow and return manifolds formed in 22-mm or 28-mm copper tube. It is advantageous in a bungalow to connect all the radiators to a single pair of manifolds located close to the boiler. In a house of one or more storeys it will be more convenient to install a pair of manifolds on each floor, siting them in the most central and accessible position so that the length of the 8-mm-diameter copper circuits to the radiators can be kept short to save material and reduce frictional resistance to a minimum.

It cannot be emphasized too strongly that all calculations for microbore (the term most widely used now) must be determined correctly because the design for this system is more critical than for smallbore.

Figure 26A Layout for a typical open-tank system

Figure 26B Layout for a typical sealed-tank system

The advantages of microbore can be summarized as follows:

(a) The installation time is reduced, providing a cost saving.
(b) The disturbance of a household is confined to a minimum during installation.
(c) A reduction in the cost of materials used.
(d) A more flexible installation which permits extension at a later date.
(e) A reduced water content which provides more sensitivity to thermostatic control.
(f) A faster heat recovery is achieved.

Design and installation of microbore

Copper tubing for microbore installations is manufactured to BS 2871, Part 2 and it is available in 6 mm, 8 mm and 10 mm outside diameter. The tube is supplied in coil lengths of 10 m, 20 m, 25 m, 30 m and 50 m and it is of soft temper which permits easy manipulation by hand, or pipe-bending springs if sharp radius bends are required. The soft-temper tube reduces the noise level in the system which occurs with high velocities.

The manifold could be described as the heart of the microbore system. There are a number of patterns available, one of which is called the 'Microfold' manufactured by the Wednesbury Tube Company. This component is fabricated from a length of copper tube with a disc brazed in the centre, thereby providing both flow and return chambers in one unit. To this length a number of stub bosses are soldered which have compression fittings to which the microbore tubing is connected.

Three patterns of Microfold are available:

WM18 designed for use with up to nine radiators and a maximum capacity of 26 kW.
WM12 for up to six radiators and a maximum of 17 kW.
WM8 constructed of 22-mm copper tube having provision for up to four radiators of 11 kW.

The ends of the Microfold are to half-hard temper to allow the use of compression or capillary fittings. A special spanner is supplied to fit easily between the stub bosses when making connections.

Double entry radiator valve

The double entry radiator valve is intended to complete the termination of the twin microbore tubes at one tapping on the radiator, making a neat unobtrusive connection. The valve has a BSP taper thread which screws into the radiator. The twin outlets are designed to take 10-mm tube.

During the installation it should be noted that the flow connection is nearer to the radiator and the return is into the valve body. In operation the valve controls the return from the radiator.

When using this valve with standard single panel radiators a length of 10-mm tube is fitted to the valve and inserted into the bottom waterway of the radiator for return circulation. The length of this tube should not be less than 180 mm. In the case of double panel radiators, a special flexible insert is necessary to negotiate the header of the radiator. This flexible insert must be used in all double panel radiators.

When fitting microbore tubing, a length a little more than the distance between the manifold and the radiator is uncoiled and then cut with pliers to ensure that the ends of the pipe are closed together to prevent the ingress of extraneous matter. When preparing the pipe for jointing it must be cut with a fine-toothed hacksaw and the burrs removed with a fine file.

As already stated, the nature of the copper tube facilitates the bending and fixing of microbore. New methods of pipe clipping are being used and a number of clips and cover strips are available. It is sufficient however to restrict the clips to parts where the tube is exposed and needs to be secured down the side of window frames or along the skirting board. The cover strip gives the neatest finish to tubes prominently in view. The flow and return pipes can often be installed without disturbing the normal working of the house, a fact very much appreciated by the householder.

In new houses, a plastic coated microbore tube can be buried in the plaster, eliminating the need for other protective measures. Care must always be exercised in running out the coil of tubing to protect it from sharp edges which could kink the tube and affect the performance of the heating circuit.

On completion of the installation, the whole system should be washed out immediately to ensure that no foreign bodies remain in the tubes. Some form of inhibitor should be added when recharging the system.

Sealed systems

All wet heating systems are operated by the continuous recycling of water by means of a pump through the boiler and radiators or unit heaters, and it is of paramount importance that only minimum water replacement should take place. However, following the principle of the Perkins system, engineers in America and on the Continent have, for many years, been using a sealed-tank method by which loss of water from the system is virtually eliminated. There is therefore little need for periodic 'topping up' and a mains supply through a ball valve is not required.

Sealed expansion tank

In a closed system it is essential to install, at a convenient point in the circuit, a sealed expansion tank (sometimes called a flexible membrane vessel) which is just large enough to take up the expansion volume when the temperature rises (see Figure 27). The vessel is normally of a welded steel construction into which is fitted a flexible diaphragm dividing it into two compartments, one of which is filled with nitrogen or air, and the other with water from the heating system: the absorption of air into the water – which occurred with the Perkins system – is thereby prevented. The air or nitrogen cushion is pressurized to support the static head created by the height of the water in the system so that the original gas volume remains unchanged when the system is filled up. When the boiler is fired and the water temperature rises, expansion of the water pushes back the diaphragm and compresses the nitrogen or air on the opposite side, causing an increase of pressure throughout the system.

With all sealed systems, the optimum size for the vessel is dependent upon the water capacity and the working temperature of the installation. A range of flexible membrane vessels is available and the manufacturers should be consulted regarding selection.

Figure 27   Expansion tank with flexible diaphragm for sealed system. (A) Before the boiler has been fired the tank contains only air or nitrogen. (B) As the temperature rises the diaphragm moves to accept the increased water volume. (C) Position of diaphragm when water temperature has reached its maximum.

Location of sealed expansion tank

As the sealed expansion tank is comparatively small, it can be placed at more or less any convenient point in the system, and this obviously makes concealment relatively easy. Where there is a possibility of tanks being isolated when valves are shut off many installers position the expansion tank close to the boiler. If an air purger fitting, which consists of a simple air separation and float-type air vent, is used, venting can, if required, be a semi-automatic operation. Installation costs can be reduced by fitting a combined sealed tank and air purger unit. If the layout of the pipework is such as to make it more convenient for the sealed tank and air purger units to be installed separately, this will not impair the efficiency of the system, but it is recommended that the air purger should be at the point of highest temperature and therefore as close to the boiler as possible. To gain full economic advantage from the sealed system the average water temperature should generally be higher than for the open-tank system. However, there are many sealed-tank installations in use working at a mean temperature of 78°C, the average for open-tank systems.

The Economy 7 boiler

The Economy 7 boiler is produced by Heatrae Sadia and marketed by the Electricity Council to be installed either as an initial system of heating or to replace a boiler in an existing system.

Briefly, it is a rectangular water-storage tank with heating elements located in the bottom to heat water using Economy 7 rate electricity. Additional elements are located at the top to boost the heat during the day as necessary. The boiler comes complete with integral pipework, insulation, control box, mixing valves and pump (see Figure 28).

There are three standard sizes (though special requirements are made to order and boilers can be erected on site) as follows:

E7 680 litres' capacity for property with heat loss of 4–6 kW.
E7 900 litres' capacity for property with heat loss of 6–8 kW.
E7 1350 litres' capacity for property with heat loss of 8–10 kW.

Working head is 7.2 m measured from the base of the boiler to the water level in the feed and expansion tank.

Loadings for 680 litres' capacity are 12 kW element for night and 9 kW for day. The temperature controller uses platinum resistance elements and solid-state control circuitry, and temperatures are pre-set to the following:

22 mm connection for open vent

pressure relief valve

heaters with thermostats

15 mm

flow to radiators

Danfoss Kovm mixing valve with Ravi sensor

check valve (anti gravity)

22 mm

valved pump

15 mm return and gate valve

22 mm cold feed

heaters with thermostats

insulated tank

outer casing

drain cock

Dimensions (of outer casing)

height 2100 mm
width 610 mm
depth 915 mm

Figure 28 General view of 680 litre Economy 7 boiler

	House °C	Bungalow °C
Night store temperature	98	92
Day elements	70	70
Limit temperature	103	97
Return water temperature	40	40

The system works by heating the storage during the night-time off-peak period, then heat is distributed in the normal way by pumping hot stored water, mixed with return water, through the radiators (see Figure 29A). The stratification of the water in the storage vessel ensures a stable flow temperature throughout the day. A common-size boiler is one with a capacity of 680 litres, which is adequate for a house with up to about 5.5 kW heat loss.

Ideally the boiler should be fitted within the dwelling where any heat loss from it will be of benefit, but it can be fitted in any practical location – garage, outhouse, etc. – providing it is adequately protected against low temperature and the pipe runs are not over-long.

When using the Economy 7 boiler as a replacement unit it is advisable to disconnect, or valve off, any existing domestic hot-water storage cylinder and primary flow and return pipework as the heat loss from gravity circulation can be considerable. Furthermore, in summer there would be standing losses from both the main storage vessel and the domestic hot-water cylinder at a time when only domestic hot water is required. These losses would generally absorb more energy than would be used to provide hot water (see Figure 29B). Towel rails connected to the primary flow and return should be disconnected and piped to the pumped circuit.

For domestic supplies an Economy 7 hot-water cylinder should be installed which works on exactly the same principle as the boiler. Hot-water draw-offs should not be taken from the boiler.

Whatever the heating system, it is beneficial to have the property insulated: for heat-storage systems it is essential. Particular attention should be paid to roofs, cavity walls, external doors and windows, remembering always, however, to provide adequate ventilation to prevent (among other things) condensation.

single storage unit

two units in parallel

Figure 29A

A — Separate the gravity feed HWS from space heating. This could be achieved by valving-off the run of pipe between the coil feed and system expansion (at the point marked X in the diagram). A better method would be to disconnect the feed and return from the indirect coil and then blank off the open ends (marked || on the diagram). Economy 7 water heating can then be installed.

B — Replace boiler with Electric Boiler connecting vent and cold feed directly to unit.

C — Replace F and E tank if necessary.

NB — broken line shows original boiler and gravity feed HWS.

Figure 29B

*Figure 29C
With the door off,
the long-life Incoloy
elements at the top
and bottom of the
Heatrae Sadia
Economy 7 domestic
control heating
boiler can be seen
clearly*

Figure 29D
Superseven cylinder
manufactured by IMI
Range for Economy 7
operation

Feed and expansion tank

The Economy 7 boiler requires a feed and expansion tank exactly the same as any other heating system, apart from the primatic system. It should have a capacity to water line of 18 litres plus 6 per cent of the volume of water in the system. Therefore, a system containing 780 litres (680 litres for the storage unit plus 100 litres in the pipes and radiators) would require an expansion vessel with a capacity to water line of 65 litres.

8
Plumbing Fitments in the Home

The kitchen

Sinks

The kitchen sink, from the days when it was made from brown earthenware and about three inches in depth, has now become an attractive as well as functional piece of kitchen equipment manufactured in a number of materials and designs.

Fireclay

There are several types of kitchen sink. The once popular 'Belfast' sink, which is made of fireclay and enamelled after baking, is still used in certain areas. It is easily fixed on brackets built into the wall, or on leg supports.

Stainless steel

By far the most popular is the stainless steel sink and draining board combined, made in various sizes to suit individual requirements. The sink is stamped out of one sheet of metal, is very easy to keep clean and lends itself for use with purpose-made cabinets, giving a smooth streamlined finish (see Figure 30A).

A double-compartment sink with double drainer is made for the larger kitchen, and this is becoming increasingly popular because it enables the housewife to prepare vegetables and, where necessary to keep them in soak in one compartment while the other can be used for washing the glass, china, cooking utensils, etc. One of this type is illustrated in Figure 30B. The sinks and draining boards have a sound-deadening under-skin, and a food waste-grinding machine can be attached. Some stainless steel sinks are now made smaller and round in shape, so that no washing-up bowl is needed.

Figure 30   Types of sinks
A Stainless steel sink unit
B Double compartment sink

In most cases the back skirting of the sink is pierced to enable the hot and cold services to be run along inside a cupboard and up through the skirting, finishing with a neat chromium-plated standard and whatever type of taps that may be desired, thus giving a very clean-looking finish.

Enamelled steel

Another type is the vitreous enamelled steel sink. This is stamped out of one sheet of metal, and after colour is applied the sink is subjected to heat treatment giving the finished product a hard vitreous surface. These sinks can be obtained in various colours and sizes and, to provide the housewife with a complete unit, very attractive cabinets have been designed to match the varying colours of the sinks.

Ceramic sinks

Increasing in popularity today are luxury ceramic sinks. There is a growing selection, with choices of attractive colours, from firms

such as Ideal-Standard, all theirs being made in a strong and dimen-
sionally stable ceramic body finished in a satin glaze.

Figure 31

Food waste disposers

In the course of a year over a thousand meals (per person) may be
prepared in the kitchen of every home, not counting snacks and
in-betweens. There is nearly always some form of waste from every
type of food. This is either collected in a sink tidy or put into the bin
beneath the sink to be taken out to the dustbin (in all weathers).

There is no doubt at all that modern housewives are anxious to
improve conditions in the kitchen and the disposal of food waste is,
to some, a particularly nauseating job, i.e. cleaning scraps of food
from the sink outlet, scooping peelings from the bowl, scraping
congealed food from plates into the pedal bin, etc.

The modern food waste disposer is an electro-mechanical device fitted to the sink to macerate food waste, etc. These machines will dispose of all grades of food waste such as fish remains, fruit skins (including banana skins), vegetable parings, plate waste (including fatty materials), bones, eggshells and tea-leaves.

Installation

The food waste disposer has a 76-mm opening to the grinding chamber. This entails a 90-mm opening in the sink. Many sinks are now made with this size of opening to take either a food waste disposer or a crumb strainer waste. It is wise, therefore, if installing a new sink to see that it is one with a 90-mm opening.

Fireclay porcelain sinks of various types are now in production, with and without overflows, to take the food waste disposer.

If a stainless steel sink is already installed, it can usually be modified to take a disposer. The manufacturer of food waste disposers will lend plumbing contractors the necessary equipment to enlarge the hole and impress in it the recess for the disposer outlet. This is a simple operation for an experienced plumber.

Plumbing

All plumbing must be done in accordance with the Water Byelaws in force in the area in which the installation is to be made and in accordance with the British Standard Code of Practice COP 5572.

The proposed work must be notified to the appropriate authority before work begins. If you are in doubt about the regulations, consult the local water authority or employ a qualified plumber to carry out the work.

A deep-seal trap must be fitted to the outlet side of the disposal unit and a 42-mm waste connected with a minimum fall of 7.5° directly to the drain, or to a main discharge stack which connects directly to the drain without an intervening gully or trap. Any bend in the waste-pipe system should be of generous radius and formed without any distortion of the pipe bore.

It is most important that the waste pipe should not impose any strain on the free hanging position of the disposer. This will tend to make it noisy in operation.

All bends in the waste-pipe system should be of generous radius and formed without any distortion of the pipe bore.

Electrical

The motor incorporated in the disposer is designed to give the maximum power from a 13 A fused plug. The rating of the motor is over ¼ h.p. and is capable of a higher output over a short period. The control of the unit should be of such a nature that it conforms to I.E.E. requirements.

When running under the full load the motor takes 2.7 A, but in the event of the motor stalling under overload conditions the current taken by the motor will rise to 13 A. The circuit should therefore be fused for this current. This current will only flow for a few seconds until the overload device in the motor cuts it off. The overload protection device is a red button situated at the bottom of the motor on the waste outlet side. It is reset by pressing it firmly upwards and it will re-engage with a slight click.

The reversing feature of the appliance (if specified) is the switch below the point of the cable entry. This switch reverses the direction of rotation of the motor, thus utilizing both edges of the cutting teeth. If the reversing switch is not fitted the motor can be reversed by a qualified electrician removing the terminal cover and changing over two wires which will be exposed in the terminal block. The disposer, whilst earthed through the three pin plug and socket, should also be earthed independently.

The bathroom

Perhaps one of the most encouraging forward trends today in home life is the great interest being shown by householders in the furnishing and equipment of the bathroom. This is possibly the result of the consistent – and persistent – publicity by the manufacturers of the bathroom fitments from the bath to the tooth-brush rack. The design and quality of their products has improved and they have advertised widely and well. Public response has sharpened competition and today there is a wonderful selection from which the householder can make his choice if he decides to re-model his plumbing installation.

Baths

Enamelled cast iron

There is an attractive display of baths to be seen in the showrooms of most plumbers' merchants, baths to suit every purpose, taste and purse.

Most baths are manufactured in enamelled cast iron in various lengths to suit personal preference, available space or the decor of the house. They have flat or rolled rims and the latest shallow type has an almost flat bottom. This has many advantages over the conventional curved bath. First, the shallow 'step' makes it safe for the oldest and for the youngest members of the family. Then, with its flat bottom, it's safer for taking a shower. A shallow bath saves space and makes the bathroom look larger. One such type is shown in Figure 32.

*Figure 32
Shallow bath in
enamelled
cast iron*

Another new bath available is a porcelain enamelled one-piece apron bath. This bath has no tap holes and is supplied with hot and cold water through a spout outlet controlled by concealed valves. It must be ordered for a left- or right-hand corner as required because it obviously cannot be turned round like the normal bath with the detachable front apron.

Pressed steel baths

The modern steel bath is pressed out of one piece of steel and then vitreous enamelled. There are no feet to the bath; it is cushioned into two cradles lined with felt. The bath stands quite rigidly and it will withstand all hot-water temperatures. It is less costly than the cast iron bath.

Hydrotherapy

Nor are baths designed simply for washing. Today it is possible to enjoy the benefits of technology in the home by fitting a 'whirlpool' bath; massage by water is excellent for athletes, the elderly, and sufferers from rheumatism and arthritis; and fun for children and parents alike.

The smallest by Ideal-Standard measures 170×75 cm and will fit into any average bathroom. For more spacious bathrooms there are attractive corner baths and baths to accommodate two people.

The six impulse nozzles are adjustable and operated by a pull cord. Baths come with matching basin, w.c., bidet and shower.

Ideal-Standard whirlpool baths are supplied with the pipework for the water nozzles and aeration controls already fitted (Figure 33), and every bath is individually pre-tested. The pump is supplied ready for the plumber to fit and only two or three pipe connections (according to model) have to be made.

The electrical connections are straightforward and your electrician should provide a pull switch over the bath and a separate isolating switch.

When the pump is on, water is withdrawn from the bath through a suction outlet and recirculated through the pipework to the six nozzles below the water surface.

The aeration controls on the side of the bath may be opened to add air to the streams of water, the bubbles of air adding further liveliness to the whirlpool action.

Figure 33
Ideal-Standard's new Whirlpool
2000 system

Care of the bath

A good bath deserves good treatment before and after installation. Unfortunately, much damage can be caused before the bath is fixed. It is delivered to the site usually some time before it is installed and is left out in the weather. It is liable to damage from falling materials and rough handling. When it has been fixed by the plumber it may be scratched by other tradesmen working in the bathroom. Despite efforts by progressively minded people, it still happens that due to ignorance, stupidity and carelessness many baths are damaged. The owner of a new house will be well advised to make a close inspection of all his sanitary fittings before taking over.

Acrylic baths

Domestic baths made from cast acrylic sheet are produced by several manufacturers, and are stocked by leading builders' merchants throughout the country. Although designs and prices vary, there are some features which are common to all acrylic baths. Where coloured luxury baths are being considered, acrylic baths offer a considerable saving in cost.

Cast against plate glass, they have a superb surface finish with no ripples or blemishes. The colour goes right through the material and will not wear off. It will not stain, rust or corrode. It is unaffected by bath salts, and because it is non-porous its surface will not retain bacteria.

Light in weight

Acrylic baths weigh as little as 14 kg, saving on handling, transport and installation costs both in private houses and multi-storey buildings. Although these baths are light in weight they are completely stable once installed. A substantial cradle is provided which supports the bath both underneath and round the rim, and the cradle is included in the price of the bath. Figure 34 illustrates how easy they are to transport.

Easy to maintain

The high gloss and good appearance of acrylic baths can be preserved by cleaning with warm soapy water or detergent. When necessary mild scouring powder may be used, but some loss of surface lustre must be expected in time. This lustre can be renewed by polishing the surface with a liquid metal polish or a soft cloth. If a deep scratch is accidentally made, it can be rubbed out with a mild abrasive or, in an extreme case, with wire wool or emery paper, and the polished surface can be completely restored by rubbing with liquid metal polish.

Figure 34
One man can handle an acrylic bath

Economic

Because acrylic is a good thermal insulator, the water stays hot longer. The material is also warm to the touch. But acrylic baths are affected by extremes of heat, such as are generated by lighted cigarettes and burning matches, and these will cause marks on the surface. Lighted cigarettes should not therefore be placed on the surround or allowed to fall into the bath. Some dry-cleaning agents and paint strippers will also cause damage.

Installation and plumbing instructions

There are no special problems connected with the installation of acrylic baths, but some allowance must be made for the thermal expansion and contraction. Plumbers should pay particular attention to the fixing instructions which most manufacturers issue. In general the following points should be observed.

Installation

An unsupported acrylic bath lacks stability because of its low weight and must therefore be securely fixed to the supporting cradle which the manufacturer provides. The bath should be levelled and secured to its cradle according to the maker's instructions. The cradle should be fixed to the floor via the supporting legs of the cradle and/or to the wall along the top rear member. All surfaces of the bath cradle which are in contact with the bath are lined with felt which should not be removed or disturbed. This felt interlayer prevents creaking which could be caused by the bath rubbing against its cradle.

Creaking can also occur when adjacent side panels rub against one another at the corners or against the underside of the bath flange. The rubbing can be avoided by slightly trimming the side panels and binding the edges with cloth tape.

When the side panels are fitted to the bath cradle (see Figure 35), it is important to provide clearance holes through the panels for fixing to allow for thermal movement. Full support must be provided on the underside of the panels when drilling these holes.

When the bath is fitted flush with the wall, the final seal should be made using a silicone sealant. Small tubes of this material are available from most builders' merchants or ironmongers. For trade use there is a gun cartridge grade available – 'Silicone Building Sealant' – which is readily available from builders' merchants. Alternatively most builders' merchants or ironmongers supply a variety of specially shaped PVC strips which can be used to make the final seal.

Tiling

The walls around an acrylic bath can be tiled in the normal way following the tile adhesive manufacturer's instructions. The tiles should preferably be laid so that the lower horizontal edge of the tiling lies below the rim of the bath. In this case the tiling can be undertaken prior to the installation of the bath.

If the tiling is to be carried out after the bath has been installed, the bath should be protected to prevent accidental scratching of the surface of the bath. Some tile adhesives contain solvents which can damage acrylic and care should be taken to ensure that any adhesive accidentally falling into the bath is quickly removed. The effects of any slight surface damage may be removed by the use of a liquid metal polish.

*Figure 35
Installing an acrylic
bath*

Plumbing

When fitting the services to a bath made from acrylic sheet care must be taken to avoid damaging the material and also to avoid fitting the services in such a way that damage to the bath could occur in service.

Waste pipe

Normal sealing compounds can be used between the flange of the waste-pipe fitting and the bath, but it is recommended that a washer of some resilient material, such as rubber or polythene, be used between the nut on the underside and the bath itself. Moderate pressure only should be used to tighten the nut, care being taken to avoid excessive leverage which would occur if long-handled pipe wrenches or spanners were used.

Where a metal trap and waste pipe are used they must be accurately aligned to avoid imposing a twisting stress on the bath. It is essential to ensure sufficient flexibility in the plumbing to allow the trap and waste fitting to move with slight thermal movements of the bath otherwise there is a danger of cracking around the waste-pipe flange hole in service.

If a short length of iron piping is used, the system will be too rigid. This problem of providing resilience can be overcome by using plastics waste pipe in conjunction with a plastics or metal waste trap. The use of suitably reinforced polythene or flexible PVC pipe for the overflow connection to the trap is recommended so that the effect of any misalignment is absorbed in its resilience rather than imposed as a stress on the bath.

Taps

For the normal types of tap no special precautions are necessary other than the provision of a resilient washer between the nut and the bath.

Some types of mixer installations and hand shower fittings are considerably bigger than normal taps and, if used as grab handles by the bath occupant, could impose sufficient leverage to the bath flange to cause damage. When fittings of this type are installed they must be secured through a reinforcing member on the underside of the bath flange.

Warning

Whenever a blow lamp is being used during the plumbing operation care must be taken to ensure that the flame is kept well away from the bath.

Washbasins

It is perhaps a sad reflection on the designers of sanitary ware that many of the washbasins manufactured in this country in the past presented both the housewives and the plumbers with problems. The housewife found it impossible to keep the basin properly cleaned because of awkward corners, crevices and the bad siting of the taps, while the plumber had difficulty in fixing the services and waste pipe.

However, in recent years the manufacturers have given the matter attention and sought the help of experts in design, with the result that the new washbasins are pleasant to look at as well as being functional.

Washbasins can be obtained in glazed fireclay, vitreous china, porcelain enamelled cast iron, pressed steel and stainless steel and more recently in plastics. The range of designs is extensive – as is of course the range of prices.

A type which is becoming very popular is the *vanity basin* (Figure 36). The one illustrated has the bowl fitted flush into a plastic top having a moulded back skirting, bullnosed front edge and shaped ends. The unit has two drawers and is supported on polished beechwood legs. Another type is a basin with a spacious table top formed from square eggshell finish tiles, with a wooden cabinet beneath.

Figure 36   Vanity basin

Figure 37   A modern washbasin

Washbasins are being fitted in bedrooms and guest rooms today as well as in the bathroom and the pleasant modern types with splashbacks and mirrors will grace any room (Figure 37).

It has been suggested that wherever there is a w.c. there should be a washbasin. Furthermore, it is recommended that the tap of the washbasin should be operated by a foot pedal so that the user of the w.c. can wash his or her hands before flushing the cistern. We believe that with the attractive little washbasins now available, one could be placed in every w.c. compartment, even if it were provided with but one cold-water tap.

Water closets

The modern w.c. pan is designed to be functional, unobtrusive and easy to clean. They are available in earthenware, fireclay, stainless steel and vitreous china. There are some imported plastic w.c.s on the market.

The most commonly used type of w.c. is the washdown pedestal, so called because the flush of water washes and cleanses the whole of the internal surface of the pan. Referring to Figure 38A, the water from the flushing cistern enters the flush pipe horn and is directed round the flushing rim and then washes down the internal surface. The water seal is, of course, the barrier which prevents drain gas from entering the house.

The clanging noise of the w.c. cistern being operated and the rush of water into and out of the pan, especially at night, can be something of a nuisance. If this is a problem, it can be best overcome by the installation of a modern type siphonic w.c. pan. The seal of the trap of this type is much deeper than that of the washdown closet, thus giving a large bowl of water and a limited exposed area. A normal flush would not be sufficient to cleanse down the fittings thoroughly and leave such a large bowl re-charged with water. The contents of the pan are therefore removed by siphonic action. The action is started by the impulse of the water flush and the contents of the bowl are removed completely and silently. A typical modern siphonic w.c. is shown in Figure 38B.

Another type of w.c. which deserves more popularity is the bracket w.c. which, as shown in Figure 38C, is fixed on brackets clear of the wall, thus avoiding the joint between the floor and the pan. Because the pan is virtually fixed to the wall there is no chance of it cracking due to movement of the floor. The pan is of the washdown type.

Figure 38
A B and C
Types of w.c.s

W.C. suite of advanced design

In Figure 39 a close-coupled w.c. suite is illustrated. It is the combination of a plastic or pottery cistern with a pottery washdown pedestal w.c. pan. It incorporates a silent flush of 'hydromatic' action – a design of ducts and channels which direct the water in correct volume to the right places to effect controlled maximum flushing efficiency. The washdown pan is manufactured with the trap to British Standard specification to eliminate the risk of blockage. It is a free standing unit, only 736 mm high and projecting 710 mm from the wall. Being of low height and short projection it is easy to fit under the window in the average w.c. compartment and can be installed in many awkward places, where previously only a high-level suite could be accommodated.

The suite is available in a variety of colours and has the smooth flowing lines and shape of contemporary design in addition to maximum hygienic qualities. Even the fixing screws are domed to avoid dust-traps and the whole suite can be easily and quickly wiped clean. Two screws at the base of the pan hold the complete suite firmly in position.

The cistern in pottery or plastic is non-corroding; it bolts directly to the pan without need for brackets or flush pipe. An easy pressure on the cistern handle will immediately operate the polythene siphon mechanism to give a positive action flush.

The w.c. is fitted with an attractively shaped seat which has been designed to blend with the contemporary lines of the whole suite. It is made from what the manufacturers claim to be a virtually unbreakable material. The seat is flexible and needs no buffers. It has a light, smooth surface which is very easy to keep clean. The material from which it is made is a bad conductor of heat, therefore the seat is not as chilly as some other types.

It is a simple matter to fix the seat by means of its adjustable sliding bolt with wing nuts and washers. There are no hinge rods to be cut as the fixing bolts are adjustable in the socket.

The hinges are streamlined to make them easy to wipe clean. The seat has a cover made from strong flexible material which overlaps it, thus completing the streamlined appearance of the suite.

Figure 39
A close-coupled w.c. suite

Toilet aids to the aged and infirm

Manufacturers of plumbing appliances are always ready to co-operate in producing gadgets and aids to help the aged and infirm. Three such aids are illustrated in Figure 40.

Figure 40   Toilet aids for the infirm
A   The 'Seataid'
B   Bath safety seat
C   Bath safety rail

The bidet

This is a sanitary fitting designed on lines similar to a pedestal w.c. pan, but is intended primarily as an ablution fitment for use by women in matters of personal hygiene. It is used in a great many homes and hotels on the Continent, and is now in demand in this country. It should be used only for ablutionary purposes and therefore may be connected to a waste pipe and not a soil pipe.

Figure 41 shows a modern type of bidet. It is provided with a douche jet in an upward direction for ablution, and this is controlled by hot and cold valves. The bidet does not have a seat and warm water can be used to flush the fitment so that the rim is rendered comfortable to the person sitting on it.

IMPORTANT: The bidet must be installed in such a way as to prevent contamination of water supply. The recommended method of connecting a bidet is laid down in Section 328 (b) of the British Standard Code of Practice CP 310: 1965, which reads as follows:

Figure 41   The bidet

Appliances with submergible inlets

'Baths, washbasins, sinks and similar appliances which have not the ½" air gap between spillover level and level of discharge of the taps, mentioned in Sub-Clause 327b, and appliances with submergible inlets, such as sluicing sinks and bed pan washers as used in hospitals, laboratory sinks and bidets, should be supplied with hot water and cold water by a method which involves no danger of contamination by back flow or back-siphonage. The cold water should be supplied from a storage cistern through a separate pipe which supplies only the appliance in question or a number of similar appliances at the same level or from a flushing cistern. The hot water should be supplied from a hot-water storage cistern or cylinder by a separate pipe which supplies only the appliance or a number of similar appliances at the same level, and where a cylinder is used the pipe should be connected directly into it at a point which is higher than the appliance. Appliances are deemed to be at the same level if their water inlets are at the same level and if their spillover levels are the same, so that a range of identical bidets on the same flow level could be supplied by the same pipes, *but a bidet in a bathroom should not be supplied by the pipes supplying the bath or wash basin.'*

9

The Shower Bath in the Home

The shower is the most convenient method of bathing. It is quick, refreshing, economical and, not least important, uses constantly clean water.

Drawbacks are that you cannot soak totally immersed in supportive water, or use bath toiletries. A growing number of people are installing both baths and showers in their homes and enjoying the best that each has to offer. Showers can be fitted separately in cubicles or, if space is limited, a shower spray can be fitted over a bath.

Showers may be fitted virtually anywhere in the house providing there is a convenient hot- and cold-water supply and an accessible waste connection. There are instances of cubicle showers located on landings at the top of stairs; in the kitchens of small, two-roomed flats; and, of course, in bedrooms, where they are very convenient.

Manufacturers provide a variety of models to suit most if not all requirements. For disabled people a flat-tiled area on the ground floor with a gully outlet and easy-reach mixer valve to a spray head is ideal.

The salient advantages of the shower, not necessarily in order of importance, are:

1 It is hygienic and pleasant to use.
2 The shower is much cheaper to operate as water consumption is considerably less than with the traditional bath. This is particularly important with regard to hot water, and where water softeners are installed.
3 It follows that many showers may be obtained in succession without an increase in the heating or storage capacity.
4 The shower takes less time to use, thus alleviating bathroom queues.

5 It occupies considerably less space than a bath.
6 Because it is simple to adjust the water temperature of the shower, the possibility of a person catching cold after a hot bath is very remote, particularly if the shower is turned to cool before finishing.

First essentials

For a shower bath the hot and cold water must be mixed to give a constant supply at a selected temperature, and it is most essential that a means of varying this temperature between fully hot and fully cold should be provided. This can be done by using a mixing valve which equalizes the pressures of the hot and cold water. An obvious way of doing this with the ordinary domestic system is to arrange that the cold-water supply to the mixing fitting be taken from the same cold that feeds the hot-water system. It must be understood that byelaws prohibit the mixing of cold water direct from the main with hot water from a gravity system.

It is also essential that there is an adequate 'head', or pressure, of water at the shower itself, and this is determined by the height of the cold-water cistern above the shower outlet. Generally, it can be taken that if the bottom of the cold-water cistern is a minimum 3 m above the floor of the bathroom, a satisfactory shower can be obtained. If a greater height than this is possible, so much the better. If the cold-water side of the mixing fitting is fed from a single pipe from the supply cistern it will avoid the possibility of other draw-off points causing a drop in pressure and a consequent sudden increase in temperature at the shower.

Mixing fittings

These are divided broadly into two classes: (1) the mixer, which consists of a pair of orthodox hot and cold screw-down taps with their outlets joined together by means of a 'breeching' or mixing chamber; and (2) the mixing valve, which combines the two taps or valves in one, is operated by a single control handle, and allows any temperature between hot and cold to be selected manually by moving a pointer round a scale marked 'cold', 'tepid' and 'hot'.

With the mixer fitting no visual indication of the temperature is given, and this, allied to the fact that two valves have to be adjusted, makes it slower and very much less convenient and positive than the mixing valve.

There is a wide selection of mixing valves on the market today, attractively designed with durable, easy-clean finishes suitable for any bathroom.

All hot- and cold-water supplies to shower mixers or mixing valves should be from storage cisterns to ensure equal operating pressures, though some valves incorporate compensating valves which make it possible to have trouble-free showers even though the pressure difference is as great as 5 to 1.

The following specifications and illustrations are reproduced by courtesy of Barking-Grohe.

The Neotherm CP brass shower uses a sealed capsule thermostat to control the hot and cold supplies, ensuring that the shower never varies from the selected temperature. The wax-capsule thermostat is unaffected by corrosion or deposits from hard water. Hot surge is eliminated by the provision of a special metering device. The temperature selector is clearly seen when the user is under the shower, and the Neotherm has special compensating valves for controlling the pressure of hot and cold supplies. It is suitable for use with the Main Severn instantaneous water heater.

Figure 42
Neotherm thermostatic shower

The Euromix CP brass concealed shower mixer has a single lever regulator for precision control of volume and water temperature, provided that the hot and cold supplies are at a constant pressure and temperature. Supplies can come from above, below or from the sides.

Figure 43
Euromix single lever shower mixer

The Crystal CP brass deck bath-shower mixer with non-rising headworks has a button for changing to 'shower' which is conveniently positioned on top of the nozzle, and the diverter returns automatically to the 'bath' position when the water is turned off. Accepted by the National Water Council.

Shower booster

For a normal shower installation a nominal head or gravity pressure of 1.5 m (effective head 1 m at a flow rate of 0.1 l.p.s.) is recommended.

However, in many homes space is not available to install a cold-water cistern high enough to achieve the recommended head and flow. In such cases the Barking-Grohe Flomatic shower booster permits the use of a shower where it would otherwise be impractical. By lifting the water available at the mixer, the booster can provide a flow of 0.1 l.p.s. with a water supply that would otherwise provide as little as .03 l.p.s. flow at the shower rose. It can accomplish this when the water level in the full cistern is a mere 200 mm above the highest point of the shower attachment.

Figure 44   Flomatic shower booster installation

It does not pressurize the flow (which would require some three times the volume of water than is normally available in British domestic installations). To ensure an effective shower it is important that the Flomatic is not starved of water. The flow of blended water available at the shower outlet of the mixer (with shower attachment) should be at least 6 l.p.m. For bath/shower mixers with self-return diverters the flow should be at least 8.4 l.p.m.

Hot- and cold-water supplies to the shower mixer or bath/shower mixer must originate from a cold-water cistern (see Figure 44): the Flomatic must not be connected to high-pressure mains water. The maximum pressure on one side of the mixer should be 7 metre head. The Flomatic has been designed for use with domestic water at 40°C (50°C max.) and like other Barking-Grohe products should be used only in approved plumbing installations.

Shower rose or shower spray

The part of the shower fitting from which the water finally issues may be referred to as the shower head and is available in two types. There is the 'rose' type, often referred to as the 'watering can' type. This can take different forms but in each the water comes out in jets from a large number of small holes. The advantages of the rose are that it will operate at a somewhat lower head of water and, if large enough, can give an extremely heavy shower; it is often slightly cheaper in cost than the sprayer.

The other type of shower head is the 'sprayer', which, by utilizing centrifugal force, forms a spray of what might be likened to rain-drops. The sprayer makes use of a small number of comparatively large holes. Much more economical in the use of water, its consumption is predetermined. Its centrifugal action has the effect of assisting the mixing of hot and cold water, and its small consumption will damp down sudden variations of temperature that may be caused by 'heavy-handed' manipulation of the mixing valve handle. The spray of aerated drops is extremely pleasant and invigorating. The most popular type passes 7 litres per minute, of which only half is hot and half cold. The sprayer is much less liable to choke up, can easily be cleaned out and is almost indestructible in use. It usually has a cap end that can be changed to vary the volume and size of spray.

The shower in conjunction with the bath

Practically any type of shower can be used over a bath. For the sake of convenience and safety, the type of bath which has a fairly wide and flat bottom is to be preferred. It is also an advantage if the bath is fixed in a corner or in an alcove, and is of the type which has a flat rim, or roll, over which the walls will project slightly, thus ensuring that water cannot run between the bath and the walls.

In order to prevent water from the shower spraying or splashing over the front of the bath on to the floor, some type of shield is required. This may take the form of a glass panel which can be hinged to swing outwards, or, as is more usual and considerably cheaper, a curtain rail and waterproof curtain can be used. The curtain will need to be long enough to fall inside the bath, and wide enough to cover the whole length of the bath. If the bath is fitted in an alcove, a straight rail of tube with a flange at each end will be required. If the bath is fitted in a corner, the rail will need to be semi-rectangular, and the 'return' end, across the bath, will be secured to the back wall. In this case the curtain must be wide enough to draw across both the front and the return end.

In the case of a bath which stands clear of the walls, a curtain rail of fully rectangular shape can be provided. Curtain rails of circular form are obtainable, but although they permit a person to stand under the shower, they allow insufficient space for soaping and rinsing.

It is usual to fix the shower at the end above the bath taps and to take the water supplies to it from the service pipes feeding the latter. Both mixer fittings and mixing valves are made in 22-mm size, and arranged for the double purpose of filling the bath and feeding the shower, as required. It is more common, however, to provide a separate 15-mm mixing valve for the shower and a pair of 22-mm taps, or a 22-mm mixer fitting, for the bath.

Whatever the arrangement may be, it must be remembered that, so long as mixing takes place and the hot water comes from a low-pressure storage system, the cold-water connection must not be made direct to the main.

NOTE: Flexible hoses to shower heads from bath mixer taps must be fixed in such a way as to prevent the spray nozzle from falling into the bath below the spillover level of the fitting.

In-line showers

Available on the market are electric in-line heater units for shower heads connected to a mains water supply. Before considering the use of this type of heater, both the local water authority and the Electricity Board should be consulted.

The shower bath as a complete unit

Where the shower is to take the place of, or is to be separate from, the slipper bath, a shower cubicle can be built in as an annexe to the bathroom (see Figure 45), or in any other suitable place in the house. The essentials here are a receiving tray at floor level, which can be obtained in fireclay, enamelled iron, stainless steel or fibreglass. The tray may also be of tiled construction or built from timber and lined with a suitable material. A 42-mm waste and trap and an overflow connection will be required. Three walls can be tiled or rendered waterproof by other suitable means, and the fourth, or front, side can be provided with a waterproof curtain sufficiently long to fall inside the receiving tray. Curtains are now available in plastics, in a large range of attractive colours and patterns. Shower enclosures can also be built of glass panels with metal framework.

The shower fitting itself can either be of the 'overhead' or 'shoulder height' type, the latter allowing a person to take a shower without necessarily wetting the hair, or adjustable-height shower heads are available.

Figure 45
Built-in shower cubicle

Figure 46
Prefabricated shower cabinet

Completely prefabricated shower cabinets with plinth, receiving tray, front curtains, mixing valve and shower head are available. These can be set anywhere in the house – even on a bedroom carpet – and only require connecting up to hot and cold supplies and waste pipe. No building work of any kind is required. They can be purchased in dismantled sections, allowing them to be taken upstairs and through narrow doorways, to where they can easily and quickly be assembled. It is preferable that cabinets of this type be provided with a top to them, as this helps to confine the vapour that rises from a shower. It is also important that they should be rustproof. For this reason the use of aluminium is of great advantage for it cannot rust and is very light to handle. This type of cabinet is illustrated in Figure 46.

The absence of a domestic hot-water supply system does not rule out a shower. Showers can be operated from certain types of gas and electric water heaters, and can then utilize pressure direct from the cold-water main. Mixing arrangements are available for such showers, and, as both hot and cold come direct from the main, regulations are not contravened.

One maker of self-contained shower cabinets supplies them complete with either gas or electric water heater, and a tapping is often taken from the same heater to supply hot water to a nearby washbasin.

Children almost invariably love showers, but in the case of very young infants it is advisable to have the waste of the receiving tray fitted with a tubular 'standing' overflow which will allow the water to build up to the level of the top of this tube before overflowing. This makes a very satisfactory bath for infants. One make of aluminium shower cabinet on the market is fitted with this type of standing overflow which permits a depth of approximately four inches of water to build up in the receiving tray.

Installing a shower

A shower can be installed in a space as small as 760 mm square. In fact, this often makes it worth while installing a shower as an extra washing facility.

The 'head' or pressure of water

If a 'U' tube is fed from the underside of a water cistern (Figure 47) and the open end of the 'U' tube is at the same level as the level of the tank, no water will flow. If a metre is cut from the open end of the 'U' tube then the water will flow and a small fountain of water will spray from the end of the 'U' tube. If we now cut 3 m from the open end of the 'U' tube it can be appreciated that water will try to reach its own level and create a much higher fountain.

The amount that is cut from the tube is known as the 'head' or pressure. In the first instance we would have had a 1-metre head and in the second instance a 3-metre head, and the greater the head the faster the flow and the more water available.

Figure 47
'Head' or pressure of water

Installation

No shower fitting can work satisfactorily unless the installation is right. Careful attention to the following simple requirements is needed only once, and will ensure many years of trouble-free service.

Measure the head

Make sure that there is sufficient head or pressure available. You must position the shower rose at a minimum distance of 1 m below the base of the cold-water cistern (Figure 48). (You can ignore the position of the hot-water cylinder on the hot supply; it is its source, as cold water, that matters.) This is the absolute minimum figure and will probably only be acceptable where pipe runs are short and a gentle wetting shower is acceptable.

Normally the figure should be 1.5 m or more which should provide a spray of 4.5–6.5 litres per minute. However, where even the figure of 1 m is impossible to achieve a booster can be installed.

Where the gravity flow is insufficient, a shower booster is the answer (see Figure 44).

Figure 48
Recommended 'head'

see note below

cold water
hot water
cold water
hot water

NOTE: 1.5 m is the recommended height from the underside of the cistern to the shower rose. If the pipe runs are short this may be reduced to a minimum of 1 m.

Equal pressures

Hot- and cold-water supply pressures to the shower controller need to be about equal. If, as is most likely, the hot-water system is fed from a storage cistern, then the cold-water supply to the controller **must** come from a cistern. It is technically wrong and dangerous, and contrary to the byelaws of water authorities, to connect the hot-water side of the controller to the cistern and the cold-water side to the mains supply.

Get the flows right

Eliminate long lengths of pipes in which static hot water rapidly cools and that infuriating wait while tepid water issues from the shower rose.

You should also note that the connections with existing pipe runs which feed other taps or draw-offs could lead to intermittent water starvation and so to fluctuations in the shower temperature. Ideally it is better to run independent hot- and cold-water supplies to the controller from the hot-water storage cylinder and the cold-water cistern. The elements of a satisfactory household system are shown, with the pipe runs to the shower.

All controllers are fitted with a maximum temperature limiting device which will enable you to set the maximum temperature of the spray to suit your particular requirements. Hot-water boilers can be set at different temperatures for various purposes and this will affect the shower temperature. The maximum temperature limiting device is an essential safety feature when boilers installed for the dual purpose of central heating and water supply are set at maximum temperature.

10
Soil- and Waste-Pipe Systems

The owner of a house should know something about the system used to dispose of waste water and human excrement from his home. His personal comfort and that of his family is dependent to a great extent on the efficient working of this disposal system. It matters very little to him what happens to the waste matter after it has passed from the plumbing system of his home, although he would in fact probably find it a surprisingly fascinating subject.

The house is a small self-contained unit, one of many thousands connected by a drainage system to the town sewer. This chapter is concerned only with the system within the house.

Definitions

A *waste pipe* takes the discharge from bath, washbasin, kitchen sink, bidet, washing machine and dishwashing machine.
A *soil pipe* takes the discharge from the w.c. pan.

As with water supply, there are specific byelaws which regulate the installation of soil and waste pipes.

Exclusion of foul air

Despite the fact that present-day medical evidence discounts the once predominant opinion that drain gas can give rise to epidemics and is detrimental to health, there is no person who would want foul air to penetrate his home. The smell of drains is obnoxious and it is imperative that it should be sealed off at all the appliances used for excremental, ablutionary and domestic purposes. Protection against drain gas infiltration is attained by that simple appliance called a trap. A trap is formed by a depression or a U-bend which will retain water in the trap but not interfere with the flow of water through the pipes. Traps may be separate fittings or embodied in the appliance itself. In Figure 49 a P-trap is illustrated. The important part of the trap is the water seal, which forms the barrier against the passage of drain air through the trap. While that seal is maintained all will be well but if the water level is depressed below the point marked 'dip' on the illustration, then drain gas can infiltrate into the house. Traps are fixed to kitchen sinks, washbasins, bidets and baths and are an integral part of the w.c. pan.

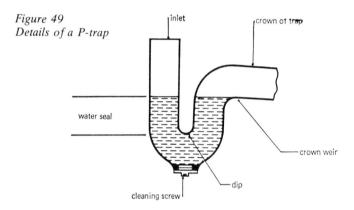

Figure 49
Details of a P-trap

Loss of water seal of a trap

The loss of the vital water seal of a trap may be due to one or more of the following reasons:

1 Self-siphonage.
2 Induced siphonage.
3 Evaporation.

The chief problems are to avoid self-siphonage, by which individual appliances suck out their own seals when they discharge, and induced siphonage by which the discharge of one fitting 'pulls' out the seal of another fitting.

In long spells of hot, dry weather the evaporation of a trap may occur if a house is left unoccupied for any length of time. The only remedy is to arrange for someone to flush the appliances from time to time.

Single-stack plumbing

The system of sanitary plumbing being installed in most new houses is known as 'single stack', so called because all the fitments of the house discharge into a single pipe and no vent pipes are connected

to the individual appliances. The purpose of the system is to reduce
the complexity and cost of plumbing.

The efficiency of single-stack plumbing depends on the close
grouping of the fitments and keeping the length of branch pipes to a
minimum. Careful attention to design and installation procedure is
essential and the basic requirements must be observed.

The Building Research Station has produced a Digest (No. 80)
setting out its recommendations on single-stack plumbing and these
should form the basis for any such installation.

The design curve shown in Figure 50 gives the gradients of waste
pipes from washbasins. The risk of self-siphonage from washbasins
is much more closely dependent on the design of the branch connection to the stack than it is for other appliances. The diameter of the
bore of the pipe, and its length and fall are all important factors.
Waste pipes from washbasins being of relatively small diameter
(30 mm) run fully charged and by doing so cause suction at the trap
end of the discharge. This can be remedied by limiting the length
and slope of the pipe. Figure 50 gives maximum allowable slopes for
varying lengths of nominal 30-mm waste pipe used in conjunction
with a 75-mm-seal P-trap.

Figure 50
Design curve for nominal 30-mm
wastes and 75-mm-seal P-traps
connected to single BS lavatory
basins. The minimum desirable
slope is 20 mm. (The slopes
recommended are allowable
maxima but the pipes need not
be fixed at exactly the gradients
read off the graph.)

Figure 51
Design of single-stack
system – main features

If the basin is more than 1.68 m from the stack suction at the trap can be reduced if a short tail piece of 30-mm pipe discharges into a 40-mm or 50-mm pipe connected to the stack. This will prevent the pipe running full.

Self-sealing traps are available and these avoid the complete self-siphonage of the discharge by permitting some of the waste water to drain back to reform the trap seal.

S-traps and small radius bends in the waste pipe should be avoided wherever possible as they tend to increase self-siphonage.

Water-closet branches do not run full so no matter what length they are there is no danger of self-siphonage. Nevertheless, the shape of the w.c. branch connection can induce siphonage action on branches to other appliances in the stack. The w.c. connection should be swept in the direction of the flow (see Figure 51).

BS COP 5572 recommendations

The British Standards Code of Practice 5572 recommends:

1. 32-mm wastes from basins should have a maximum length of 1.68 m. Angle of fall as determined from design curve graph (Figure 50). For basin waste pipes longer than 1.68 m the diameter should be increased to 40 mm, to a maximum length of 3 m.

2. 40-mm waste pipes from baths, sinks, showers, washing machines and dishwashers should have a maximum length of 2.4 m at 5° fall. For those over 2.4 m to a maximum length of 3 m the waste-pipe diameter should be increased to 50 mm. Sinks fitted with macerator waste-disposal units: a minimum 7.5° fall to waste pipe.

3. Any waste pipe in excess of 3 m should be vented to a safe outlet.

4. All the above fittings must be provided with a 75-mm deep-seal trap.

5. Each fitting should be connected separately to the main discharge stack.

6. Over-long waste pipes should be avoided. They are noisy in operation and sediment is likely to accumulate.

7. Bends in waste pipes should be kept to a minimum. If there's an excessive number on any one branch it may require to be vented. All bends must be a minimum 75-mm radius to the centre line.

8. Any raking or vertical drop in the waste run and the pipe should be increased in diameter.

9 Adequate access points should be provided on all waste branches, particularly at changes of direction.

10 W.c. branches should be swept in the direction of the flow with a minimum radius sweep of 50 mm. W.c. branch pipe connections up to 6 m long have been used successfully when laid to very shallow falls.

11 The bend at the foot of the stack should be a minimum radius of 200 mm. For heavily loaded stacks, longer-radius bends are obtainable, or two 135° bends can be fitted together. The vertical distance between the lowest branch connection and the invert of the drain should be at least 760 mm. (Ideally, all ground-flow fittings should discharge to drain, especially where the house has been converted to flats.)

12 To avoid back pressure there should be no offsets in stacks below the topmost appliance unless pressure-relief venting is provided. Offsets above the topmost fitting are permissible.

   On stacks with low loading factors, local authorities may often allow offsets made with high-angle bends (minimum 135°), providing that the topmost bend of the offset is at least 750 mm below the branch immediately above it.

NOTE: Code of Practice recommendations are usually accepted by local authorities but they are subject to local conditions and byelaw requirements. Consultation with the local council's inspectorate is advised before any installation, replacement or repair work is undertaken.

BS 5503

The production of w.c. pans has been rationalized to provide a level spigot outlet. This saves manufacturers having to produce many variations of each model: P-trap straight; P-trap left-hand turn; P-trap right-hand turn; S-trap; and so on.

   The modern level-outlet pan is connected to the branch soil pipe by means of either a 90° bend connected to form either an S-trap or side turn outlet, or a 104° connector to form the traditional P-trap pan.

   In the case of a P-trap or side turn pan the BS requires a 14° fall from the outlet of the pan and care should be taken to ensure that the appropriate adaptor is fitted to the proper angle.

   Many level-outlet pans are incorrectly jointed with straight connectors, which may result in washback of the pan's contents after flushing.

Comprehensive designing based on practical research

The Marley Plumbing team who carried out practical experiments and developed their findings into practical designs and fittings, have given valuable advice to plumbers through the media of lectures and publications.

The collar boss

One intriguing development in single-stack plumbing is the Marley Collar Boss. This soil-pipe fitting has been designed to overcome a number of different installation problems which occurred when the Building Regulations required all soil pipes in new construction to be located inside buildings.

BS COP 5572 recommends that small-diameter branch wastes with orifices of connections exposed to the w.c. discharge do not join the soil pipe in the 200-mm area below the centre of the w.c. branch (see Figure 51). This often means that the bath waste pipework has to offset through the floor and enter the stack via a boss branch fitted below or in the ceiling space.

Apart from increasing the labour content of the plumbing installation a bath waste passing down through the floor can create structural difficulties for other building trades.

The collar boss has an annular cavity in the main body which receives water from the branch wastes and this is deflected down and around the sloping shoulders into the vertical stack. Air always present in the annular chamber removes any tendency for self-siphonage to occur while the effluent is flowing from the branch waste and the normal rate of discharge from the sanitary fitment is unaffected. Discharge from the w.c. is prevented from making contact with the annular space or boss connections by the wall of the internal socket. Details of the collar boss are given in Figure 52A.

Figure 52   The Marley Collar Boss

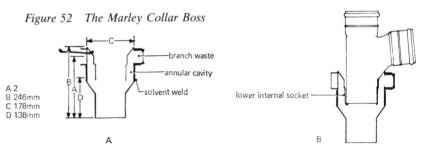

Figure 53   Complete installation of collar boss

The intermediate pipe clip is an injection moulded uPVC component. This acts as a guide for the vertical pipe. Support for the soil system is provided by the mild steel plastic coated socket clip. The length of pipe in the vertical stack and horizontal branches will vary with different contracts. The appropriate dimensions may be obtained from the construction drawings in each case.

The local ring seal joint on the boss branch allows for movement when hot-water waste is discharging into the stack, and the anchor rib on the socket locating the clip ensures that the pipework is adequately supported.

If required, a straight access pipe may be fitted in the vertical stack.

It is important to provide an expanded expansion joint between fixed points on all uPVC soil and waste pipes. Manufacturers' instructions on method and position should be followed closely.

w.c. adaptor

bent w.c. connector

collar boss

socket pipe clip

single boss branch

pipe solvent
,socket

drain adaptor

Installation of the collar boss

When the collar boss has to be fitted high up under the throat of a 100-mm branch the spigot of the branch may be solvent-welded to the lower internal socket (Figure 52B).

Care must be taken when using the collar boss in conjunction with any of the 100-mm boss branch fittings in the soil-pipe range not to close up (by shortening the spigot end of the junction) the centre-to-centre dimension of the opposing bosses to less than 110 mm for branch wastes up to 50 mm, or to less than 200 mm for 100-mm branches.

In Figure 53 a typical domestic installation is shown. Detailed diagrams and catalogue about the fittings may be obtained from Marley Extrusions Ltd, Lenham, Maidstone, Kent ME17 2DE.

Council approval must be obtained before using the collar boss system. Some authorities, especially those in Inner London, may not approve a fitting that is not readily accessible for cleaning, while others may need to be satisfied that alternative direct connections to stack are not possible.

11
Rainwater Disposal

In years gone by the house-builder had little regard for rainwater pipes or gutters. They were necessary however, and the main thing was to get them fixed as cheaply as possible – after all, you could hardly sell a house on its rainwater pipes and gutters! Even on better-class, architect-designed properties, very little thought was given to the position, size or design of rainwater pipes and gutters. Many a house having a commanding or attractive elevation has been spoiled by a festoon of pipes and gutters.

Cheap materials, bad sizing, and inferior fixing of rainwater gutters and pipes has caused damage to property. Leaking joints, pipes and metal gutters fixed without painting, and in a position so that painting the back of them has been impossible, has caused them to rust away after a relatively short period of time.

Need for care in fixing

The purpose of a rainwater gutter is to catch all the rain falling on the roof during the heavier downfall and to convey it to the outlets, where it empties into the down pipe, which in turn should be capable of conducting all the water to the drain, without any spilling out of the joints and soaking the brickwork.

All joints must be made properly and if the pipes and gutters are of metal they must be painted. They should be fixed in such a manner that it is possible to clean them and repaint them at regular intervals. Gutters must have an adequate fall to take the water to the outlets and to make them self-cleaning. It is essential that the outlets of the gutters should be protected with wire balloons to prevent leaves and other matter from choking the downpipe.

Plastics rainwater goods

Possibly the most progressive development has been the design and supply of plastics rainwater goods, which provide many advantages over those made from other materials.

By using plastics materials it has been possible to employ greatly improved design techniques resulting in a considerably improved appearance and substantial savings in erection costs. Guttering is simply snapped into a bracket which has a moulded-in clip joint and a butyl rubber strip provides a 100 per cent watertight seal. In this way the need for gutter bolts has been removed.

Plastics have eliminated corrosion problems – a constant worry with cast iron. Hence there is no need for surface protection and for this reason the guttering and downpiping can be self-coloured.

A comprehensive guide to rainwater gutter and downpipe installation follows. It is intended for the installer and the householder, explaining step by step the procedure and techniques. For simplicity we have restricted the instruction to one type only manufactured by Marley Plumbing Ltd.

Figure 54

The most serious losses occasioned by a failure of conventional guttering and downpiping are due not only to corrosion but to accidents through storage and transportation, and breakage during fitting. The percentage of breakages with plastics rainwater goods is negligible, and their lightness in weight makes transportation and erection on site a simple and trouble-free job.

Gutter installation

The Marley gutter joint with separate jointing strap located between notches on spigot and socket is shown in Figure 54. The strap compresses the spigot down against the synthetic rubber seal which is secured in every socket before the products leave the factory. When correctly assembled the joint cannot pull apart, and it will absorb the expansion and contraction of the gutter while maintaining a watertight seal.

Position of the underground drain

The location of the underground drain is an important factor in setting out a gutter installation. The trapped gulley or drain socket at ground level automatically determines the centre line of the gutter outlet which is normally immediately above. This is shown in Figure 55.

Position of rainwater pipes

Considerations affecting the position of rainwater pipes are:

1 Architectural requirements.
2 Maximum flow capacity of the gutter.
3 Underground drainage design.
4 The accuracy with which the timber fascia is fixed to the rafters.

Item 4 is particularly important yet often overlooked. Fascia boards that are not level cause a large gap to develop between the gutter and the eaves' course of tiles (see Figure 56). This occurs when the plumber is fitting to gradients which are opposed to the slope of the fascia.

Fixing the brackets to a timber fascia

Plumbers occasionally fix the brackets and install the gutter before the roof is tiled. There is a risk of damage to the PVC gutters during the roof tiling operation as well as a great accumulation of debris collecting in the gutter. It is advised that the sequence of events be arranged that the roof is tiled and the final painting of the fascia board completed before the plumber fixes the brackets and installs the gutter while the scaffolding is still in position. A good plumber can be relied upon not to damage the finished paintwork while fixing the gutter. The brackets may be fixed in the usual way with a string line acting as a guide to alignment for brackets between the extreme end of the installation and the outlet of the gutter (Figure 57).

Figure 55

When fitting brackets to a fall, the end bracket at the high point should be secured as close as possible to the underside of the roofing felt and projecting eaves' course of tiles. The intermediate brackets are then screwed to the fascia with zinc plated or sheradized round head screws at a maximum of 1-m centres (Figure 58).

Figure 56

Figure 57

Figure 58

Figure 59

Position of gutter brackets

Gutter is supplied in 3-m lengths and on long straight runs the arrangement of brackets should be as indicated in Figure 59. The gutter union has a centre portion to accommodate the fascia bracket and this feature in combination with the 3-m double spigot lengths of gutter, provides the method of arranging the support brackets. Careful attention to detail is necessary because the union bracket has to be accurately located taking into account the small tolerance on every gutter length.

Figure 60

Angle

External and internal angles should have close supporting brackets on each side of the joints as shown in Figure 60.

Outlets

Gutter outlets should also have brackets fitted on each side of the joints to the gutter (Figure 61). The stopend outlet is designed to suit the fascia bracket and this type should always be installed so that the rainwater pipe may be correctly engaged with the nozzle of the outlet.

Fitting and jointing the gutter

Lengths of gutter are introduced into the brackets as illustrated in Figure 62 and clipped into place under the projection at the front of the fascia brackets. As the gutter is installed the rear edge should turn into the brackets under the roofing felt in order that the gap between gutter and tiles is weathered. This prevents the rainwater from being blown against the fascia as it runs from the tiles into the gutter.

Figure 61

outlet

outlet

roofing felt

Figure 62   *Figure 63*

To assemble a joint, clip the gutter strap around the socket of a fitting between the notches. Turn the spigot end of the gutter into the socket, under the back edge of the strap, so that the retaining projection fits into the notch (see Figure 63). Ease the front edge of the gutter spigot down until it snaps under the strap. This now compresses the gutter against the pre-fixed synthetic rubber seal to form a watertight joint.

Finally line up the notches on the spigot and socket so that the strap is in the centre (Figure 64).

Cutting and notching the gutter

Occasionally it will be necessary to cut a length of gutter. A fine tooth saw should be used for this purpose taking care to cut straight at 90 degrees to the axis of the gutter (Figure 65). The notches must then be cut or filed into the edges of the spigot end. A tool is available from the Marley Company for cutting notches but they can be done quite easily using a file. The dimensions of the notch are given in Figure 66.

The notches must always be formed before attempting to complete a joint.

Figure 64

Figure 65

Figure 66

Circular pipe installation

Connection to the gutter outlet

When the gutter outlet is positioned directly above the drain, the offset must be of the correct projection passing straight back under the soffit to engage with the rainwater pipe. Ideally a ring seal should be located in the socket recess of the offset to secure and seal the connection of the two fittings (Figure 67).

Solvent-welded offsets

An offset may be fabricated on site from an offset socket, offset spigot and an offcut of pipe. The procedure is as follows:

1 Cut pipe to length and remove all rough edges (Figure 68A).
2 Internal surfaces of solvent-weld sockets and outside of pipe ends should be wiped perfectly clean with a dry cloth.
3 Assemble the offset dry and draw pencil lines along the pipe and fittings (Figure 68B) to ensure correct alignment.
4 Remove pipe from fittings. Apply solvent cement evenly around the spigots and inside sockets from the tube (Figure 68C).
5 Press pipe and fittings quickly and firmly together taking care to line up with pencil guide lines.
6 Leave the offset for several minutes before fitting into position in order that the joints may set properly.

Figure 67

*Figure 68
A and B*

offset end

A   offset end

A

pencil lines
or use mould
lines on fittings
for guide to
alignment

B

ring seal

tube of solvent cement

Figure 68 C

Connection of offset to rainwater pipe

The offset spigot is 112 mm long. This allows the socket of the offset to be pushed fully on to the nozzle of the outlet, while providing some facility for adjusting the first pipe clip. The clip is fastened around the socket, then the offset and first length of pipe are placed in position (Figure 69).

If the holes in the pipe bracket backplate fail to come in line with a mortar joint, *do not* lower the offset on the nozzle of the outlet. Instead, measure the amount of spigot to be cut off, in order that the pipe clip may be fixed in the next joint up.

Location of rainwater pipe clips

Pipe clips are provided to fit both the rainwater pipe and the pipe socket.

The vertical centres of pipe clips are usually marked on the wall with the aid of a plumb line suspended from the top pipe-clip position.

Pipe-clip backplates, or in the case of the one piece fitting, the clip itself, are secured to the structure with two 38 or 32 mm × 10 gauge zinc plated or sheradized round-head steel screws. Purpose-made fibre or plastics plugs should be inserted into the fixing holes when they have been drilled. The use of handmade softwood plugs should be avoided (Figure 70).

Figure 69

trim spigot of offset to allow pipe clip to be secured in mortar joint

Figure 70

The pipe clips are supplied with nuts and bolts to fasten the uPVC ring to the backplate. Every rainwater pipe should have a clip located at the socket to support the pipework system. Intermediate pipe clips should then be provided in the centre of each pipe length where it exceeds 2 m.

An expansion gap of 10 mm should be left between the end of each pipe and the bottom of the socket (Figure 71).

Figure 71

mark spigot end
to ensure expansion
allowance is provided

10mm
expansion gap

Connection to the underground drain

Depending on the design of the system of buried drainage, rainwater pipes may terminate as follows:

1 Below the grating level of a trapped gully, providing access to the gully is not obstructed for cleaning purposes. This problem can be overcome if a short length of pipe is removable immediately above the gully mouth. The grating should be cut to fit snugly to the pipe, which must be terminated above the water line of the trap.
2 Connected to the back or side inlet of the gully with a 2:1 sand and cement joint.
3 Connected direct to an untrapped bend with a 2:1 sand and cement joint or with an adaptor. This is permissible only if the gutter outlet discharges to air in a 'safe' position: 900 mm above or 3 m from the highest opening in the building.

The gutter (half-round) described in this chapter is only one of many designs available. The range includes Deep Flow, an elliptical gutter 110 × 75 mm deep, which, when running full, has a capacity equal to a 150-mm half-round gutter.

Fixed level with an outlet at one end, it has a flow capacity of 1.83 l.p.s.; fixed level with an outlet in the centre, its flow capacity is

3.43 l.p.s. Flow capacity is increased by at least 20 per cent when fixed at gradients of 1:600 or more.

Assuming the maximum rainfall intensity at 75 mm per hour, a Deep Flow gutter fixed level with an outlet at one end will drain a roof of 87 sq. m (167 sq. m with an outlet in the centre). Fixed with a gradient of 1:600 and an outlet at one end, it will drain a roof of 105 sq. m (200 sq. m with an outlet in the centre).

Figure 72
Connection to the underground drain

Therefore, a typical terrace of five houses, having a frontage of 37.5 m and a roof pitch of 5 m, can be adequately drained by a rainwater pipe front and back sited in the centre. This gutter may be used in conjunction with a Deep Flow Box Eaves unit and either 68-mm-diameter round rainwater pipe or 65-mm-square pipe.

For full details of fittings range, capacities, discharge rates, etc., the appropriate catalogues issued by Marley Extrusions Ltd should be consulted.

12

Plastics Plumbing

Plastics, although with a history of over a hundred years, is a comparatively new material in the plumbing world. Because of its lower cost in both material and labour it has moved in rather rapidly, with the result that information relating to these materials has not been digested quickly enough.

Another danger that has arisen is that various types of plastics can be used for the same application, but require different techniques for installation and jointing, just as do copper and stainless steel. Therefore, it is essential for the plumber to recognize these new plastics materials.

The plastics range of material today is vast, but, for practical purposes, only the materials that are used for plumbing products are our real concern. The main emphasis must be on the plastics that make up the pipe and fittings of the installation and not so much the plastics materials of the appliance to which the system has to be connected. The reason being that individual items under the categories of storage and flushing cisterns, taps, basins and baths, generally have their own specific fixing instructions attached.

Five groups of plastics

The plastics that are used in the manufacture of pipes and fittings for above and below ground drainage and services, can be placed into five basic groups.

1 Polyvinyl chloride (uPVC and CPVC).
2 Styrene based (ABS).
3 Polyolefin (polyethylene and polypropylene).
4 Glass reinforced plastics.
5 Nylon.

Group 1 is used for rainwater, soil, waste, overflow below ground drainage, cold-water services and pressure pipe installations. Has a hard, smooth finish with a specific gravity of approximately 1.4.

Group 2 is used for waste runs generally of 35 mm, 42 mm and 54 mm nominal bore diameters, overflow pipes and water services. Is being used in the US for soil installations, but not in the UK. Similar appearance and feel to the plastics in Group 1, but with a specific gravity of approximately 1.1.

Group 3 is used for waste runs including laboratory work, overflow, water services and internal rainwater systems. Has a 'waxy' feel about it, and a specific gravity of 0.9 to 0.96.

Group 4 is used for rainwater roof outlets, valley type gutters and special fittings for large-diameter pipework. Can be recognized by the glass fibre reinforcements embedded in the material. Its specific gravity is 1–2 or more, depending on the glass content.

Group 5 is used sometimes for 'minibore' central heating tube and pressure pipework. Has a similar feel and appearance to the polyolefins and a specific gravity of approximately 1.1.

Identification of plastics

It will be observed that out of these five groups, only the polyolefins (Group 3) has a specific gravity of less than 1.0. Hence by placing a fitting, or small offcut from the pipe in fresh water, only the items made from material in this group will float. It is essential that no air is trapped in the components when carrying out this procedure.

Both the components from Groups 1 and 2 will not float, but they can be distinguished apart by offering small shavings of the materials to a flame. The polyvinyl chloride in Group 1 will be self-extinguishing when taken away from the flame, while the styrene based material in Group 2 will continue to burn.

As already mentioned the glass reinforced plastics in Group 4 can be identified by the glass fibres embedded in the material, but as a further test press a hot metal point on its surface. Resin glass material will only char slightly whereas the effects on Groups 1, 2, 3 and 5 will be similar, only in a lesser degree, to a hot metal point pressed on to sealing wax.

The nylon plastics can be distinguished from Group 3 because they will sink in water and not burn so readily. The vapour smell when burnt is akin to burning hair.

Identification of all these plastics components by their colour is not possible, because depending on the pigments used in manufacture, a variety of colours can be produced.

It is important to be able to identify these plastics materials that are used for pipes and fittings, for each group has certain individual characteristics. For instance, chemical resistance, temperature limitation, weathering ability and coefficient of expansion present each group with a different specification, which must be taken into consideration. Identification is also important to ensure that the correct method of jointing is applied.

In practice it has been proved that all joints of recognized design which incorporate a seal ring are suitable for making an air- or watertight joint with all plastics piping. But the method of making a joint by using a solvent to fuse the materials together is limited to specific plastics.

The polyolefins and nylon plastics cannot be solvent-welded, whereas the styrene based and polyvinyl chloride materials can. Different formulations of solvent cements are supplied for the two latter groups and should be used in accordance with the manufacturers' instructions.

With the exception of the comment on nylon, we have refrained from identifying the materials by burning and smelling the vapour, for it is felt that some experience in this field is required to ascertain positive results. Also any foreign matter in the burnt plastics could mislead one's sense of smell. It must also be noted that inhaling any vapour given off from smouldering plastics may be injurious to health.

In constant association with these materials the plumber will quickly be able to recognize the polyolefins and resin glass easily by the appearance, feel and the manner in which the saw cuts them. Distinguishing between the styrene based and polyvinyl chloride is a little more difficult and very often the experienced person has to apply a basic identification test to confirm the result.

Once the identification of the plastics materials is established the recognized methods of working can be applied.

Allowance for expansion

If expansion is not allowed for a rigid plastics pipework, there could be a high percentage of failure in the installation, but the degree of failure could depend upon the use to which the system is put.

For instance, if the ambient and flow temperature of the pipe varies by say, only 10°C, it would be debatable whether the installation would suffer any damage, even if the length of the rigid pipe run was 1.5 or 2 m.

In practice it is very seldom that these conditions can be guaranteed for the life of the installation. Therefore, maximum temperature conditions relating to the purpose of the system should always be assured.

When a rapid and a reasonable amount of ex ansion is taking place, the cause is generally due to very hot fluid flowing through the pipe. In these conditions plastics pipe would be more vulnerable to deformation, and unless adequate allowance is made for expansion, the pipe is likely to buckle. It could also damage or disturb the fittings locating the pipe.

Changes in surrounding temperatures also create thermal movement, especially with outside pipe and gutter installations.

Plastics plumbing installation

Manufacturers of plastics pipe and fittings systems issue their own fixing instructions and it is always advisable to conform to their recommendations. The allowances for thermal movement have been established, not only by theoretical calculations, but by sound practical testing.

A question that concerns many is that if an installation could be constantly moving throughout its life, surely this would be detrimental to the system? The answer is simply that if the system has been fitted to give adequate allowance for freedom of movement then under its normal working conditions for which it was designed no strain will be taking place, and the material will not be subjected to fatigue.

Obviously there will also be expansion and contraction movement in the width of the pipe work. But as this is so slight it can be disregarded for practical purposes.

With plastics piping there is a considerable temperature difference between the discharge and the outside wall of the pipe. A clear example of this is illustrated in the British Standards discharge cycling test for uPVC soil pipes. This shows that when 35 litres of water at 91°C are discharged into a 3.17-mm-thick uPVC soil stack from a waste entry, over a period of 90 seconds, the hottest point of the outside pipe wall will be in the region of 70°C. Because the material has low heat transmission, the expansion of the pipe is not so great as one would expect in relation to the high temperature of the discharge. It is for this reason that plastics systems will withstand intermittent discharges of higher temperatures than the melting point of the material.

It will be seen from the foregoing that the main concern about thermal movement in plastics is related to rigid materials, which are being widely used for above surface drainage.

Soil and waste pipes

We are going to deal only with soil, waste and drain pipes because it is in this area of plumbing that most progress has been made in the use of plastics. The tried and tested material used is unplasticized polyvinyl chloride which we will now refer to as uPVC. These pipes have been widely used in the UK for some years now and they are accepted by almost every local authority. Changes and improvements in design of components and materials are constantly taking place and the wise plumber will keep abreast with these changes by maintaining regular communication with manufacturers and trade bodies through technical literature and meetings. He should also concern himself with British Standard Code of Practice for the material and the Digests published by the Building Research Station. For comprehensive information of a practical nature he can obtain publications from the Institute of Plumbing: 64 Station Lane, Hornchurch, Essex RM12 6NB.

Types of systems

The uPVC systems for soil pipes are classified by their methods of jointing and are placed in two groups: (1) joint ring and (2) solvent weld. The joint ring systems may include fittings in the range where a solvent weld is required and similarly solvent weld will require expansion joints in the form of joint ring sockets to allow for thermal movement. A typical joint ring system is illustrated in Figure 73. There are a few other types all of which are effective and suitable.

Joint ring systems

The joint ring illustrated fits in the annular space of the pipe socket. When the other pipe is inserted in the socket, a coupling nut locks the ring on the socket and spigot surfaces, forming a gas and watertight seal.

It is important to know that the design of ring seals differs from one to another manufacturer and they are seldom interchangeable. It is essential that the correct ring be used and that the manufacturer's instructions be carefully followed. Even when the joint rings are despatched from the manufacturer already fitted into the sockets, the plumber should carefully check to see that the ring is correctly engaged and undamaged before he makes the joint.

When the ring is supplied separately it should be cleaned before being inserted in the recess in the socket, which of course should also be cleaned.

Figure 73

Joint assembly

There is a very wide range of soil- and waste-pipe fittings available in the plastics industry and most manufacturers can provide the plumber with lavish brochures showing their complete range and giving detailed dimensions and fixing instructions.

One general point which must never be overlooked in assembling plastics pipes and fittings is the maker's instructions giving the depth to which the spigot should be inserted in the socket. These instructions are in some cases given on an adhesive tape attached to the spigot of the fitting. In other cases the depth is indicated by a mark on the spigot end.

In all installations the spigot end of a pipe secured by a joint ring should always be directed in the same line as the flow of water from the appliance.

Spigot ends must be chamfered to permit easy assembly. Moulded fittings have their spigot ends already chamfered but the plumber must prepare pipe ends himself.

Plastics pipes can be cut with a hacksaw, or better still, a fine-toothed saw. With the latter it is less difficult to make the absolutely square cut so important in correct assembly of pipes and fittings.

When the pipe has been cut a pencil guide line should be made around the pipe about 7 mm from the end. Then with a fine rasp or a coarse file a chamfer can be formed working from the guide line to the end of the pipe, avoiding making a sharp edge.

The pipe must be inserted in the fitting to the correct depth and this can be achieved by marking with a pencil the depth recommended by the manufacturer or, alternatively, the pipe may be inserted to the full depth, marked with the pencil and then withdrawn 10 mm. A bold line is then drawn round the pipe at the top of the socket (see Figure 74). This method provides a better guide line for preparing the pipe for assembly with the socket.

Figure 74

Figure 75

Making the joint

The chamfer on the spigot is lubricated generously with silicone grease, and with the clean joint ring in place in the cleaned socket, the spigot is lined up with the socket. With a slight twisting motion the spigot is pushed firmly past the joint ring and into the socket until the insertion depth mark is level with the face of the socket.

Coupling-nut compression type joint seal

The compression type of joint is made by a locknut which is slipped on to the spigot end after which the joint ring is also put on the pipe end. The spigot is then entered in the socket to the prescribed depth and the joint completed by pushing the rubber ring into the socket and tightening the locknut. The manufacturers of this type of joint issue explicit instructions which must be followed in all assembly work.

Solvent-weld system

The solvent-weld system is satisfactory providing that due allowance is made for thermal movement in the installation. This is achieved by the use of expansion joints of the ring seal type at strategic points.

In a solvent-weld joint the spigot should fit very closely with the socket. In some cases it will be found that when pushed together dry, the spigot will enter the socket only to about half its depth but when the solvent is applied its effect will allow penetration of the spigot to full depth.

With the solvent-weld system it is permissible to make a joint against the direction of the flow in vertical and horizontal pipework installations (see Figure 75). There are all-socketed fittings and fittings with spigot ends to which the pipes are attached by using loose sockets. When properly made the joint is homogeneous and rigid with the spigot butted against the internal shoulder of the socket, leaving a smooth, full and uninterrupted pipe bore.

Care must be taken to make a solvent weld correctly and the procedure is as follows:

1 Remove any dust and swarf from the pipe end and the socket, both of which should be cleaned thoroughly. The manufacturers of plastics supply a special cleaning fluid which acts as a degreasing agent and removes the glossy surface from uPVC in readiness for the solvent welding operation.
2 If a pipe has to be cut the end should be square and even and all rough edges smoothed before applying solvent.
3 Apply one coat of uPVC solvent cement to the external surface of the spigot and the internal surface of the socket.
4 Push the spigot into the socket with a slight twisting movement until it reaches the full depth of the socket.
5 Wipe off any surplus solvent cement immediately.

With careful treatment it should be possible to handle the joint in two or three minutes. If possible, however, the system should be left to stand for 24 hours before being put into operation.

Some manufacturers recommend the application of two coats of solvent cement.

13
Copper Tubes

The resistance of copper to corrosion is due to the formation by natural processes of a protective film which in nearly all cases renders the metal safe from attack by the atmosphere and from any water, gas or soil with which it may be in contact. The film is primarily an oxidized layer which forms a protective skin on both the outside and inside of copper tubes and ensures not only a long life for the pipe, but also that it will not contaminate drinking water or require any additional treatment for protection when installed in contact with the usual building materials or normal types of soil.

Copper tubes cannot rust and do not require painting, which saves cost and, in the case of hot-water pipes, avoids the unpleasant smell of warm paint. In certain cases where the pipes are run on the surface the attractive appearance of the metal can be exploited to fit in with the surrounding decorative features. The trend in modern plumbing is to conceal pipes as much as possible, with the result that they are installed in chases or are buried in walls and floors. Concrete, lime and lime plasters and cement mortar have no harmful effect on copper but there are certain acid soils and materials which are known to be corrosive to all metals.

In addition to their corrosion-resisting properties, copper tubes possess a combination of physical characteristics. The ductility of the metal enables them to be manipulated with ease, while the strength of even light gauge tubes ensures that they will withstand pressures far higher than those to be found in normal pipe services. They will withstand considerable internal and external pressures and adjust themselves to irregularities and settlements in soils or buildings without risk of fractures occurring.

In certain cases, tubes are subject to expansion and contraction due to changes in temperature, and restraint of the consequent movement at various points in the installation may set up stresses in the pipes. Copper combines sufficient strength and elasticity to prevent any permanent deformation such as that which occurs in tubes of softer metals under similar conditions. In the case of heating installations carried out in copper tubes, there is economy in the amount of metal used, with a consequent saving in cost, weight and space, a smaller mass of metal to be heated, less radiation surface for heat loss, thereby effecting a saving in fuel. The ease with which the tubes can be handled, manipulated and jointed means lower labour costs and reduction in the number of fittings required.

The very smooth surface of a solid drawn copper tube is an important feature particularly in a water pipe, because of the low frictional resistance it offers to the flow of the water, and in waste pipes because it reduces the risk of blockages to a minimum. In hard-water districts the calcium carbonate deposits do not adhere so quickly or firmly to the smooth interior surface of a copper tube and therefore the removal of scale that might form is a simple matter.

From a decorative point of view, the smooth non-rusting exterior surface has much to commend it and it can be polished easily and it readily takes a plated finish. The small diameter tubes and fittings give a neat and unobtrusive appearance.

A point of some importance arising from the smooth bore of a copper pipe is that, in conjunction with the strength and ductility of copper, it gives a measure of protection against frost bursting. It is of course not claimed by the manufacturers of copper tubes that they will not burst under extreme conditions. A good plumber would never expose any tube installation to extreme conditions.

An important development came with the manufacture of long-length copper tubes in 'dead soft' temper. These tubes are supplied in coils of 20 m.

Jointing copper tubes

The present widespread use of copper for all forms of pipework in plumbing is a result of the development of suitable means of jointing light gauge tubes. The joints commonly used today in house plumbing are manipulative and non-manipulative compression fittings and capillary joints.

British Standard 864, Part 2: 1971 'Capillary Fittings and Compression Fittings of Copper and Copper Alloy, for Use with Light Gauge Copper Tube' gives the general dimensions and classifies them as non-manipulative compression fittings Type A, manipulative compression fittings Type B, and capillary soldered fittings, and states that the fittings shall be of copper or a suitable corrosion resisting alloy. A table sets out the allowable hydraulic working pressures and temperatures for these forms of joints, but it may be of interest that many of the fittings, both capillary and compression, can be used at higher temperatures and pressures. Under such conditions, however, the manufacturers should be consulted regarding any special requirements necessary to ensure their products give satisfactory service.

In the past some confusion has arisen over the method of stating the sizes of tees or crosses. To overcome this a standard method has now been adopted by all manufacturers as follows:

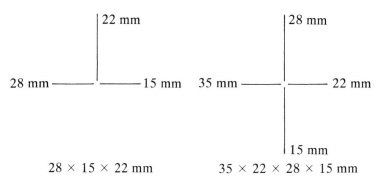

$$28 \times 15 \times 22 \text{ mm} \qquad 35 \times 22 \times 28 \times 15 \text{ mm}$$

A good type of joint should not in any way restrict the bore of the tube and in addition should preferably be so made as to allow easy dismantling for maintenance or other purposes.

Compression joints

The non-manipulative compression joint, as the name implies, does not require any working of the tube end other than cutting it square. The joint is made tight by means of a loose ring or sleeve which grips the outside wall of the tube when the coupling nut is tightened.

In the manipulative type of compression joint the end of the tube is flared, cupped or belled with special forming tools and is compressed by means of a coupling nut against the shaped end of corresponding section on the fitting or a loose thimble.

Figure 76 shows typical joints of the non-manipulative type. A joint of this type is made by slipping the coupling nut and compression ring on to the squared end of the tube and inserting it into the mouth of the fitting up to the internal shoulder. The coupling nut is then screwed up tight with a spanner, causing the edge, or edges, of the compression ring to bite into the copper tube. The effect (A) is shown in exaggerated form.

Figure 76   Non-manipulative compression joints

In Figure 77 are shown three main types of manipulative compression joints. Joint No. 1 is prepared by cutting the tube to length, squaring off the end and, after slipping the coupling nut on, a special expanding tool is inserted into the tube. A tommy-bar in the tool is then turned in its housing to the stop; by this action the steel balls in the tool are forced outwards and at the same time are rotated, thereby swageing a bead in the tube wall. The tool is removed from the tube by bringing the tommy-bar back to its original position. The tube is then inserted in the mouth of the fitting and the joint completed by screwing up the coupling nut.

In joint No. 2, the centre ferrule is machined from copper, bronze and brass and the angle or degree of taper matches that formed on the tube end after it has been expanded by the steel drift. The mouth of the male portion of the fitting and the friction ring inside the coupling nut are similarly machined, so that the jointing faces all marry up. The union is assembled by screwing up the coupling nut with a spanner, the body of the fitting being held at the same time with another spanner.

In preparing joint No. 3, the coupling nut is first slipped over the tube end, a split collar die is placed on the tube and secured by tightening up the side nuts; the tube end is then opened by the drift Z and after withdrawing this, the second drift Z is used to form the belled or cupped mouth as shown. The collar is removed by unbolting and the tube end pulled up tight to the body by screwing up the coupling nut, thus making a mechanically sound joint.

Figure 77   Manipulative compression joints

Capillary-soldered joints

Since the soldered or sweated joints – or as they should be called – capillary joints were introduced in this country, development has been taken up on a considerable scale and now the joint has come to be generally accepted as neat, sound and economical. Capillary fittings are suitable for hot- and cold-water services and waste pipes. They are made from copper and copper alloys.

Capillary fittings are constructed upon the basic principle of capillary attraction, which provides the means by which molten solder is drawn into the narrow space between the two closely fitting metal surfaces of the exterior of the tube ends and the interior of the jointing piece. The joint can be made either in the horizontal or the vertical position. The closeness of the fit is the main factor in ensuring capillary attraction, and it is therefore of the greatest importance that the fittings are those intended for the exact gauges and diameters of the tubes being used.

The certainty of an exact fit is provided for by the British Standard for Light Gauge Copper Tubes (BS 2871: Part 1 and BS 864: Part 2) which specifies both wall thicknesses and external diameters and states the permissible tolerances; and is still further assured by BS 864, Part 2: 1971 'Capillary Fittings and Compression Fittings for Use with Light Gauge Copper Tubes', which similarly specifies the dimensions of fittings.

It was thought at one time that there might be a likelihood of corrosion due to electrolytic action taking place between the copper of the tubes or fittings and the jointing solder. This fear was unfounded, however, for it is most unlikely that any appreciable action could take place with normal waters and a properly made joint, since the amount of solder left exposed to the action of the water inside the pipe, or to condensation on the outside, is so small as to be negligible. If the water is likely to be of such a corrosive nature that there is a danger of electrolytic action, it may be assumed that it is sufficiently corrosive to act upon plain metal and should therefore be submitted to preliminary examination no matter what type of joint is used.

However, the presence of other dissimilar metals in the system may produce electrolysis, which may make otherwise acceptable water aggressive. One effect of this could be an attack on the lead content of any solder accessible to the water, which could increase the lead content of the water above the safe levels. For this reason, end-feed lead solder joints should be omitted from pipework carrying water for drinking or culinary use. Compression fittings should be used instead.

Years of experience have now proved that capillary joints are perfectly satisfactory for hot water and heating installations. Where especially long pipe runs are encountered in such installations, provision should be made to take up the movement due to temperature variations, by means of expansion bends or expansion joints. These are hardly ever likely to be required for installations in the ordinary dwelling house.

Assembling capillary joints

The assembly of any type of capillary joint consists, briefly, of cutting square the tube ends, thoroughly cleaning them and the inside of the fitting, fluxing, inserting the tubes in the fitting and heating with a blowlamp. When heat is applied, solder is fed into the joint from solder wire applied (A) at a touch hole in the fitting, (B) at the mouth of the fitting, or (C) from a reservoir of solder already within the fitting. These fittings are illustrated in Figure 78. As an alternative to feeding solder in by these means, the joint can be made with solder paint, applied evenly to the tube after cleaning and prior to inserting in the fitting.

Figure 78
Capillary joints
for copper tubes

Much emphasis is placed on the need for close attention to every detail in making capillary joints even though it appears to be a very simple process. The steps are as follows:

1 The tube must be cut square to sit evenly on the shoulder at the bottom of the socket, and all rough edges formed by the sawing operation should be removed by file or reamer. For sawing, a special vice is obtainable which has interchangeable jaws to hold tubes of all sizes. The vice holds any length of tube, and because the saw blade moves between close guides, there is less burr to be removed and no trueing up is required after the cut is made.

2 The exterior surface of the tube at its ends and the interior surface of the fitting must be scoured to remove all traces of dirt and oxide, which would prevent the solder from adhering to the metal. This operation should be carried out with steel wool or sandpaper but emery paper or emery cloth should not be used.

3 The metal surfaces to be united on both tube and fitting are next evenly coated with flux to prevent the surfaces from oxidizing when heat is applied. It is most important that the flux used should be one approved by the fittings manufacturer.

4 The tube ends are then inserted in the fitting and it is important that their ends bed squarely on the socket shoulders.

5 Heat is applied by playing the flame of a blowlamp upon the outside of the socket until it has reached an even temperature all round to melt the solder evenly. The temperature may be determined when applying the solder externally (Fig. 78 A and B), by watching for flux vapours. When these appear it is time to apply the solder at the touch hole (type A) or at the mouth of the socket (type B). The socket should not be overheated, as overheating could break down the flux, oxidize the cleaned surfaces and burn the solder. In type A, if the solder does not run freely into the touch hole and does not appear at the mouth of the socket, or if in type B does not disappear freely into the socket before it finally floods up to the mouth, the joint should be regarded with suspicion and it would be advisable to re-make it.

When using type C it is only necessary to apply heat after having completed carefully the cleaning and fluxing operations. The joint should be closely inspected to check that the solder has crept out to the mouth of the socket, forming a complete and even ring of solder there.

Bending copper tubes

One of the advantages in the use of copper tubes for building services is the ease with which they can be bent either by bending machine or spring, and in the case of larger-diameter tubes, by means of sand filling, resin filling, low melting-point filler alloys or mandrel bending machines.

For a proper understanding of what is involved in bending, the reader should clearly understand what deformations take place when a copper tube is bent. The walls of a straight tube are parallel and must remain parallel after bending if the true round section of the tube is to be maintained in the bend. The original length of the tube o–o remains unaltered after bending only along the centre line of the tube. It follows that the inside, or throat, of the bend is shortened and compressed and the outside, or back, is lengthened and stretched (see Figure 79). From this it will be seen that the tube will collapse in the bend unless precautions are taken to prevent it. Therefore, it is necessary to support the tube while bending takes place. This support is provided by filling or loading the tube by the material just mentioned or by the use of a bending machine – of which there are many on the market – which will prove an economic proposition, particularly for sizes of tube up to 54 mm diameter. These machines work by hand power or through a ratchet action or gear and employ special formers and back guides to ensure that the tube, when pulled to the necessary angle, maintains its true diameter and shape throughout the length of the bend. In using any machine, the formers and guides should be maintained in good condition and well lubricated. This also applies to bending springs.

Fitting copper tubes

Advantages of light gauge copper tubes are the ease with which they can be installed and their neat appearance. These points can be appreciated where numerous tubes run parallel on walls or ceilings. They should always be accurately lined up, be parallel and plumb and kept equidistant if at all possible. The use of purpose-made fittings and bends makes this an easy matter. Where pipes change direction through 90 degrees, or are offset to pass some break or obstruction in the building, it is generally better to use bends rather than sharp elbows.

Where several pipes are running together, they should be left far enough apart to allow sufficient clearance for the securing of fixing clips.

In setting out bends or offsets, it is always worthwhile making a full sized drawing, on the bench or floor, to which the bending points on the straight pipes can be set to obtain the correct angles easily and quickly.

One additional advantage of using light gauge copper tubes is the ease with which off-site prefabrication can be done. This means a considerable saving in labour as such units can be assembled in jigs, easily transported to the site, and call for a minimum of site labour for fixing.

A   theory of bending

B   section x – x

True and deformed bends
A True bend. Each division a represents a 'throw' in making the bend.
B Deformation of bend in unsupported tubes.

to make an off-set

rule
tube

straight edge

First bend tube to required bevel and set in machine as shown. Place straight edge against outside edge of former and parallel with tube. When set to given dimension, x, bend in the usual way.

Figure 79A Bending techniques

to make double bends

square

tube

square

To bend to inside measurement,
y, mark tube as shown. Place
square on mark and insert in bending
machine so that the square touches
the inside of the groove of the former.
Bend as usual.

To bend to outside measurement,
z, mark the tube as shown.
Place square on mark and
insert in bending machine so that
the square touches the outside edge
of the former. Bend as usual.

Figure 79B Bending techniques

Copper and brass fixing clips for use with light gauge copper tubes are made in a variety of patterns.

The coefficient of thermal expansion of copper is 16.6×10^{-6}°C, that is to say a length increase of approximately 3.5 mm for every 3-m run of tube for a temperature rise of 50°C. While this amount is slightly greater than that of iron, it is considerably less than that of lead or plastic tubing. In the general run of heating and hot-water installations, the many bends and offsets which occur accommodate the amount of thermal movement that will take place due to temperature variations.

Occasional complaints of noise transmission arise as a result of high water pressures, faulty ball valves or other terminal points or where pumps or boosters are installed. The trouble can be overcome by using flexible connectors, called vibration eliminators, at terminal ends and on pump inlets and outlets. In some cases, however, noise transmission may occur as a result of inadequate use of fixing or spacing clips. Taking the Imperial measurements given in the British Standard Code of Practice CP 310: 1965 and converting these into metric terms, the fixing spaces for light gauge copper tubes are as follows:

Diameter mm	Horizontal run m	Vertical run m
12	1.2	1.5
15	1.2	1.5
18	1.2	1.5
22	2.0	2.5
28	2.0	2.5
35	2.5	3.0

Where these dimensions are adhered to, noise transmission will not occur under normal service conditions.

14
Screwed Pipes and Fittings

First it is necessary to know that the byelaws require that the pipes used shall conform to certain standards of quality. The relevant byelaw for mild steel or wrought iron pipes is a͜s follows:

'Every distributing pipe of wrought iron or steel not in contact with the soil shall comply with requirements for pipes of water (medium) quality contained in British Standard 788, 1938, for wrought iron tubes and tubulars or the requirements for Class B pipes contained in British Standard 1387, 1947, for steel tubes and tubulars and every such distributing pipe in contact with the soil shall comply with the requirements contained in the said British Standards for pipes of steam (heavy) quality and for Class C pipes respectively.'

For fittings the byelaw states:

'Every malleable cast iron fitting used in connection with any pipe to which the preceding paragraphs of this byelaw relate, shall comply with the relevant requirements of British Standard 1256/143, 1969, for malleable cast iron fittings and cast copper alloy pipe fittings.

Every wrought fitting of iron or steel used in connection with any pipe shall comply with British Standard 1740, 1951, for wrought pipe fittings and shall be of heavy weight when used in connection with steam (heavy) quality of Class C pipes.'

Protection

Unprotected iron and steel pipes are liable to severe corrosion by some waters and internal encrustation may in time be formed which will entirely close the bore of small-diameter pipes. Discoloration of the water might also occur with certain waters. All pipes should be galvanized, and where they are in contact with the soil be also coated with bitumen and wrapped with a spiral wrapping of glass tissue impregnated with bitumen. Pipes should never be fixed in contact with magnesium oxychloride flooring or with Keene's cement.

Pipe threads

The screw threads on pipes are referred to as gas threads, and the manufacturers make them to the requirements of British Standard Specification No. 21.

The screw threads on the pipes or, for that matter, all external threads are termed 'male' while the internal screw threads of pipe fittings are referred to as 'female'. It is important to use these terms when ordering fittings for any kind of plumbing work.

Pipe fittings

A very wide range of pipe fittings is available and they are manufactured in wrought iron and in malleable cast iron.

Wrought-iron fittings are products of a special process from which semi-molten metal, mixed with slag, is passed through squeezers and rolled to the desired section, from which the fittings are produced.

Malleable cast-iron fittings are cast from white iron and subsequently annealed. This is a heat-treatment process which gives the fitting a certain elasticity. Such fittings are easily recognized by the strengthening bead round the edge of the fitting. They are of pleasing appearance and because they are cheaper than wrought-iron fittings they are widely used in the plumbing trade.

In Figure 80 the range of pipe fittings available is illustrated. Those with the beads are malleable fittings. The letter M refers to male and the letter F to female. This is the method of description employed by the trade as stated earlier.

Rules for reading

It is important to know how to 'read' sizes of tee-pieces, crosses and side outlet fittings, etc.

Tee-pieces: When one size is specified it applies to each outlet, i.e. an equal tee is illustrated at A in Figure 80.

When two sizes are specified, the first applies to both ends of the barrel and the second to the branch (see B).

When three sizes are specified the first two apply to the ends of the barrel, the larger end being specified first.

Crosses: When one size is specified it applies to all the ends of the cross.

When two sizes are specified the first applies to one pair of opposite ends, the second to the other pair, the larger pair being specified first. When four sizes are specified the first two apply to one pair of opposite ends and the second two to the other pair, the larger size being specified first. It should be remembered that a cross should never be described by only three sizes.

Side outlets: When fittings have a side outlet, their ends should be specified as for normal fittings and then the size of the side outlet should be given. F in Figure 80 indicates the sequence of the size. For unequal fittings it is best to provide a sketch and indicate whether the side outlet is left or right hand in relation to the other outlets.

Figure 80   Pipe fittings

Pipe fitting

In actual practice pipe fitting consists of measuring, cutting, threading, assembling and securing lengths of pipe and fittings. Special tools are required, particularly for threading the pipes, and it is hardly likely that the do-it-yourselfer will wish to purchase them because they are expensive and are not adaptable for many other purposes. It might be possible to hire tools and equipment from a tool hire firm.

Measuring for pipework

Iron pipes should be fixed about 28 mm clear of the plaster or tiles and due allowance should be made for this when measuring.

There are several methods of measuring and these are illustrated in Figure 81.

A   End of thread to end of thread.
B   End of thread to centre of fitting.
C   End of thread to back of fitting.
D   Back of fitting to inside of fitting.
E   Centre of fitting to centre of fitting.
F   Back of fitting to end of fitting.

In all cases of measuring due allowance must be made for the engagement of the thread on to the fitting.

Figure 81   Measuring for pipework

Cutting the pipes

The easiest way to cut iron pipe is by using special wheel cutters but the pipe should never be cut completely through with this tool. It is better to make the final severance with a hacksaw thus eliminating the internal burr. For pipes of small diameter a good hacksaw has many advantages. The wheel cutters by their spreading action leave a distinct burr on both the inside and outside of the pipe and these must be removed by using a file on the outside and a reamer or rat-tail on the inside. Pipes should never be fixed without first removing the inside burr. The hacksaw cut leaves no burrs, but be careful when sawing – the blades break easily when doing this job.

Threading the pipes

There are a number of excellent stocks and dies available for threading pipe and although the finished thread made by each tool is identical, the methods of setting, adjusting and operating them differ.

It may be necessary to file a slight taper on the end of the pipe to be threaded in order to engage the dies, and good 'push-on' pressure is required as the stock is turned. Once the dies start to cut they draw themselves on to the pipe.

It is important, of course, that the dies be engaged perfectly square to the pipe so that the thread will be truly aligned. A thin-oil lubricant should be applied while the thread is being cut.

After a little experience it will be possible to decide at a glance the correct length of thread.

Connecting

Considerable care is required in assembling pipes and fittings, because a faulty joint could give a great deal of trouble and might even mean dismantling the entire system.

Before assembling, the pipes should be inspected to see that the interior is clean and free from any obstruction. If a thread has been cut then be sure that no metal cuttings remain on or inside the pipe. A sharp blow with a hammer will usually dislodge the cuttings.

To make the joint, wipe the oil from the thread with a piece of waste and then fray out the hemp and wrap it round the thread, commencing at the end and following the screw thread. A proprietary jointing paste should then be smoothed over the hemp either with a brush or by fingers.

Next, inspect the fitting to ensure that it is clean and is undamaged and it is a good idea to paint a little of the jointing paste on the thread.

The fitting must engage the pipe thread freely and it should be possible for the first few turns to be made by hand without difficulty. Then a pipe wrench should be used finally to tighten the fitting to the pipe. Gradually increase the pressure on the wrench until the fitting is really tight, but avoid over-tightening, otherwise the fitting might split.

In assembly work some fittings can be assembled in the pipe vice: others must be fixed in the location, in which case two pipe wrenches might be required, one 'holding against' the other.

Beware of a crossed thread in assembly work. This occurs when a fitting is not properly engaged with the pipe. It is easily detected by the sudden tightening of the fitting before more than a thread or two have been engaged.

After making a pipe joint, excess hemp should be removed from the end of the joint. A piece of broken hacksaw blade does this very well. Finally, any marks made by the pipe wrench should be filed off.

Pipe supports

All pipework should be supported by projecting clips commonly called 'holderbats'. The back of the holderbat may have a plate with two holes for attaching to a wood ground or may have a tail for building into the wall. The spacing of the supports should be such that there will be no sagging of the pipe, nor any possibility of it swinging on a fitting under its own weight or of being pulled by anyone.

15
Stainless Steel for Domestic Water Services

Stainless steel tube for plumbing and domestic central heating has now been in regular use since 1966 and to date many millions of feet of tubes of varying sizes have been installed.

Stainless steel is generally accepted as one of the most corrosion resisting metals available. This resistance is due to the hard, adherent and transparent oxide film that covers the surface of the metal and which re-forms instantaneously if the metal is scratched or abraded. The experience now gained in domestic plumbing confirms that the metal will remain unaffected when in contact with most types of potable water.

The tube is particularly resistant to damage because of its hardness and high strength and it requires fewer fixing clips and supports than other materials.

The clean attractive appearance of stainless steel tubing and fittings is an important advantage where they have to be fixed in view, although they may be painted without difficulty to blend with any particular colour scheme.

Dimensions and Weights of Stainless Steel Tube (BS 4127: Part 2)

Size of tube mm	Outside diameter max mm	min mm	Nominal thickness mm	Weight per metre kg	Approx. No. metres per 1,000 kg
6	6·045	5·940	0·6	0·081	12,305
8	8·045	7·940	0·6	0·110	8,965
10	10·045	9·940	0·6	0·140	7,050
12	12·045	11·940	0·6	0·170	5,823
15	15·045	14·940	0·6	0·220	4,601
18	18·045	17·940	0·7	0·310	3,283
22	22·055	21·950	0·7	0·370	2,668
28	28·055	27·950	0·8	0·550	1,829

Dimensions and weights of tube

Stainless steel tube for domestic water installations is fabricated by the continuous welding of stainless steel strip. The material used is a stainless steel containing about 18 per cent chromium and 9 per cent nickel.

Fittings

The outside diameters of the tubes are such that they can be used in conjunction with fittings specified for the standard copper tube. These fittings are manufactured from copper or copper alloy in accordance with BS 864, Part 2. Stainless steel tubes are suitable for use with capillary joints, except on drinking water services and types A and B compression fittings included in this standard. In those parts of the country where dezincification of brass fittings is liable to occur, copper or gunmetal fittings should be used and will be quite satisfactory with stainless steel. As the thermal expansion of stainless steel is very similar to that of copper there is no danger of the joints being weakened through unequal rates of expansion. Where appearance is important chromium or nickelplated copper fittings can be used.

Installation techniques

Stainless steel in contact with other metals

Care should be taken if using stainless steel in conjunction with other materials such as copper cylinders or galvanized tanks. Although, in the past, it has been generally accepted as suitable for use with other metals, some water authorities now either prohibit or discourage its use.

As with all materials used in water services, the approval of the local water undertaking should be obtained before any work is started.

Cutting the tubes

A fine-toothed hacksaw (32 teeth per 25 mm) should be used for cutting stainless steel tubes. Standard wheel pipe cutters are also suitable.

Bending

Because of its ductility the grade of stainless steel tube used for domestic water supply can be bent quite easily by an experienced plumber. The 15-mm tube can be bent by the spring method using the same technique as for copper tubes. The spring should be lightly greased to facilitate its removal after the tube has been bent.

Generally speaking, most bending machines suitable for light gauge copper tube can be used with stainless steel but experience has shown that the higher strength stainless steel requires the use of a sturdier machine than would be necessary for copper tube of similar diameters. For 15- and 22-mm stainless steel tubes it is advisable to employ the bending machines designed for copper tubes of 22 and 28 mm respectively. In case of doubt the manufacturers of bending machines will be ready to advise.

Jointing

Capillary joints

The procedure is the same as that for copper tubes and fittings (see chapter 13) but because the flux could cause skin irritation it should be applied with a spatula. Also it should be known that the thermal conductivity of stainless steel is low so heat should be applied to the fitting and not the tube.

The choice of a flux

The extremely high corrosion resistance of stainless steel depends upon its naturally occurring oxide film which re-forms immediately when damaged by abrasion. To remove it by chemical means demands a flux which must be highly corrosive at the moment when the solder is required to wet the steel to make the joint. However, the flux residues remaining after the joint has been made must not be corrosive, and therefore the acid chloride fluxes sometimes used for soldering stainless steel metalwork are not suitable for making capillary joints in stainless steel tube.

The correct fluxes are those based on phosphoric acid. This acid is sufficiently corrosive towards stainless steel at soldering temperatures to provide solder wetting but innocuous after the joint has cooled. These phosphoric acid-based fluxes in paste form, specially prepared for making capillary joints with stainless steel tubes and copper or copper alloy fittings may be obtained from builders' and plumbers' merchants.

Compression joints

Both type A and type B compression fittings can be used with stainless steel tube and the methods of jointing are explained in the chapter on jointing copper tubes.

16
Lead Pipes

Lead is the softest of the common metals and has very high ductility, malleability and corrosion resistance. It is capable of being shaped with the greatest of ease by skilled craftsmen. It does not appreciably work-harden so periodic softening and annealing are not necessary. Lead pipes can be bent into the most complicated shapes thus eliminating much jointing, and tees, crosses, right-angle turns, etc., can be made without the use of fittings.

Lead pipes for water supply

Lead is no longer an acceptable material for pipes, etc., supplying water for drinking or cooking. There is the very real danger that lead may be dissolved by water action and consequently consumed by users with adverse effects on their health.

Hard-water areas have always been considered 'safe' for lead because the inner walls of the pipe were coated with hard scale which protected the metal from any water action. It was also judged to be relatively 'inactive' when used with other metals in plumbing systems.

However, there is now evidence that lead may be vulnerable where electrolytic action takes place, and the lead content of potable water may be increased above the accepted safety level.

Existing lead systems should not be repaired or extended by using other metals. Ideally, existing lead supply pipes should be removed and replaced with materials acceptable to the local water authority. (It is worth inquiring if your local authority will make a grant to the householder towards the cost of replacing lead plumbing with another material: some do.)

Lead is, however, an acceptable (though labour-expensive) material for waste pipes, and this chapter is intended as a guide on methods of jointing, etc., for those wishing to maintain an existing system or install new.

Because it is a soft metal, it does require adequate fixing and protection. On development work there is a high risk of theft because of its scrap value.

The strength of lead

The fatigue resistance of lead is low and this must be taken into account in its method of use. Fatigue is the tendency of a metal to fail, generally by cracking, when subjected to the repeated application of stress, i.e. reverse bending, alternate heating and cooling, vibration, etc. The fixing of lead pipe is of paramount importance in preventing failure by fatigue.

Soldered joints to lead pipe

Wiped-soldered joints

Jointing lead pipes may be broadly divided into two categories: joints to distribution pipes of 10 to 40 mm internal diameter and joints to the thinner-walled soil, waste and warning pipes from 20 to 100 mm internal diameter.

The traditional method of jointing lead pipe is the wiped-soldered joint. The general procedure followed in the preparation, assembly, and the application and control of the solder, is basically similar, both for joints to the smaller-diameter distribution pipes, and for joints to soil, waste, vent and warning pipes. Greater control, however, is needed when jointing the larger-diameter, thinner-walled pipes, in both manipulating the greater mass of hot solder and in applying either the blowlamp flame or hot molten solder to the pipe walls.

To make a satisfactory wiped-soldered joint the plumber must successfully manipulate to a predetermined shape a mass of hot pasty solder which hardens rapidly on cooling. The necessary skill comes from practice.

The outline of the technique of making wiped-soldered joints given here cannot take the place of demonstration and practice, but may prove a useful guide. Some small variations in technique will be found in various parts of the country which it has not been possible to refer to here.

The dimensions of joints and the weights of solder for joints are given to indicate what experience has shown to be average good practice. It is suggested that satisfactory wiped-soldered joints need only approximate to these dimensions and weights, rather than conform to them accurately.

Table of lengths for wiped-soldered joints

Internal bore mm	Length mm	Internal bore mm	Length mm
10	70	50	80
12	70	65	80
20	70	75	90
25	75	100	90
32	75		
40	75		

Plumber's solder

The composition of standard plumber's solder is 70 per cent lead and 30 per cent tin with a small percentage of antimony in some qualities, which has a plastic range from 183 to 262°C.

Two methods of applying solder are used, the 'pot-and-ladle' and 'blowlamp' methods. The former is perhaps more suitable for repetition jobs done in the workshops, but the latter is also widely used for shopwork as well as jointing *in situ*. There is, however, no hard and fast rule, and both methods are used for all classes of work.

Characteristics of a good wiped-soldered joint

The characteristics of a good wiped-soldered joint can be illustrated with an ordinary running joint as an example (Figure 82A).

(a) A close fit at the meeting ends prevents molten solder running inside. A slight gap at the outer end permits penetration of the solder into the socket to provide a seal.
(b) The area tinned is limited by applying plumber's black to the cleaned and chalked surface of the pipe.
(c) Deep scoring with the shavehook or scriber at the outer end is avoided. The inside of the socket is cleaned. Clean tallow is smeared on the cleaned surfaces immediately.
(d) The cleaned surfaces are completely tinned.

A

underhand wiped joint
(pipes 50-100mm i/d)

ensure general heat
over whole surface

fixing point

fixing point

solder poured
on sides

B applying the solder

bring the hot solder from
the bottom of the joint

start final wiping
from the bottom

C wiping

over the back

wiping on 75-100mm pipes

Figure 82   Joint wiping

(e) The solder is applied all round in a hot creamy mass with a metallic gleam, and fully molten solder is allowed to be around the junction. Capillary action will draw the solder into the socket to help form a sound joint.

(f) The solder is formed to a smooth curve with a wiping cloth before it cools to a friable mass ensuring a solid joint. A good joint after cooling shows a bright lustre; a dull joint may be porous.

Underhand wiped joints

The procedure for preparing an underhand wiped joint with blow-lamp or pot and ladle, either on the bench or in a position of easy access, is as follows:

Cut the pipe to length, trim the ends square and remove the burr. Rasp down the spigot for socket entry. Open the socket sufficiently for spigot entry and rasp back the surplus edge. Chalk or dust the pipe ends to degrease. Apply tarnish or plumber's black. Measure scribe and shave the ends clean taking care not to cut into the pipe with the shavehook. To give a satisfactory appearance to the joint the scribed line must be at right angles to the pipe. Protect the clean surfaces with tallow. Clean inside the socket, check the entry of the spigot to ensure a close fit. Assemble the joint and fix firmly in position for wiping as shown in Figure 82b.

When using the pot and ladle, the prepared and fluxed joint is first tinned by gently pouring the molten solder on both the joint and the tarnish at either end to heat the joint area evenly. It is kept flowing in small drips or splashes on either side, and not allowed to run in a stream on the upper part of the pipe (Figure 82b). Bring up the cooled solder caught in the cloth on to the top of the joint and heat this mass up with hot solder from the ladle. Hot solder should not be allowed to fall from the bottom of the joint, but should be brought up to the top. Try to mould the solder into shape as it is applied, and start the final wiping from the bottom of the joint (Figure 82c). With a large mass of hot plastic solder the tin-rich solder will tend to drain off the bottom of the joint unless the joint is quickly cooled when completed.

For wiped-soldered joints on the larger-diameter pipes a catch cloth is used to retain the surplus solder, which will run off the joint as the operation of tinning and heating is done, and to mould the solder round the joint. The wiping cloth is used for the final operation. Using the cloth in one hand the plumber moulds the solder at the top of the joint to the required contour. With the edges kept clean the action is continued right over the back, and from slightly above bottom centre the cloth is held at the edges with both hands and brought up to the front to finish at the front near the top (Figure 82c).

Wiped joints made with blowlamp and solder stick

Joint wiping using a blowlamp and solder stick can, if the proper technique has been mastered, be a very handy method of jointing, particularly in awkward positions or confined spaces. The preparation for the joint is as previously described. The procedure is to heat up the joint and adjacent pipe with the lamp, and to rub the solder stick on the shaved area to tin the surface. As the heat is increased, the solder stick will soften and blobs of solder can be pressed round the joint. In this way the mass of plastic solder is built up all round the joint for manipulation into shape with the cloth. In wiping an underhand joint with the blowlamp the solder applied to the tinned joint is partially melted and retained in the wiping cloth while playing the blowlamp continually around the joint mainly to heat the edges and adjacent pipe walls. In moulding the joint, the cloth is first used to lift the hot plastic solder up the front and back to shape the joint roughly. The cloth is then rotated round the joint, applying a slight pressure at the edges and initially a slight side to side movement. This should result in a small surplus of solder being carried round the joint with the cloth to fill up cavities and other imperfections. When the joint is neatly shaped the surplus solder is wiped off lengthwise with a drag-off (folded strip of paper). An advantage of the blowlamp method is in readily keeping the solder within its plastic range during the wiping operation.

Wiped-soldered joints to brasswork

A joint similar to the underhand joint can be used for jointing brass liners (tail pieces) to lead pipes. These joints are required far more frequently in new work than running or branch joints.

The end of the pipe is prepared as previously described and the liner is tinned. The liner must fit closely into the opened end of the pipe and sufficient distance left between the cap and the end of the joint to allow the cap to be disconnected. The liner is secured to the pipe preparatory to wiping by inserting wooden splints; by grooving the end of the liner and closing the end of the pipe to grip into it (Figure 83b); or by burning the liner to the pipe using a suitable flux. The cap nut may be secured by screwing in a suitable bush, or with a roll of paper, which is subsequently removed (Figure 83c). Alternatively, a purpose-made tool, the burlock, can be used, which both retains the liner in position and holds the cap.

The pipe is then secured to the bench block for wiping the joint when the underhand technique as already described is to be used.

a length of tinned area

splints

b fixing the tail piece

bush to fit thread of cap nut

cap nut tied to splints

c fixing the cap nut

liner must have clearance to disconnect

groove in tail piece

temporary paper roll

Figure 83
Joints to brass liners

Rolled wiped-soldered joints

For jointing brasswork to lead pipe the rolled method is often preferred to the underhand technique, particularly for repetition work. The pipe is carefully straightened and the joint prepared in the same manner. The pipe is then supported on two bench blocks of sufficient height to permit free hand movement beneath the joint. Metal is applied to the prepared joint by blowlamp and solder stick (or pot and ladle) as the pipe is rolled slowly on the bench blocks. When sufficient plastic metal has been built up on the joint and retained in the wiping cloth, the pipe is quickly rolled towards the operative while the cloth is held at the base of the joint with a slight pressure at the edges. The cloth is removed, the joint rolled rapidly back and the action repeated to mould the joint to the required symmetrical shape. Slight pressure on the cloth will remedy any imperfections that appear. Surplus solder is then removed with a drag-off. The joint is immersed, while still hot, into water which gives it a bright lustrous appearance.

Wiped branch joints

The procedure for forming wiped branch joints for 10- to 50-mm bore pipes is as follows:

Cut and rasp down the entering branch to a spigot. Open the pipe with a small drill or pipe-opener and work up the opening to receive the branch (Figure 84A). Take care to prevent the bend-bolt driving into the inside wall of the pipe and avoid leaving a ridge below the opening. For 32 to 50-mm bore pipes the hole cut in the pipe for the entering portion is usually less than the inside diameter of the branch. Slight warming of the pipe will help to form the opening. Check the entry of the spigot carefully and ensure a close fit. The joint is scribed and shaved, with care not to cut into the pipe (Figure 84B). The branch is assembled and rigidly fixed for wiping with adequate working space all round. The joint is tinned, then the solder applied to the joint from each side, by blowlamp and solder stick or pot and ladle to obtain a general heat sufficient to maintain the solder in a plastic state. The tin-rich solder that drips down is brought up to the top with the cloth.

Figure 84
Wiped branch joints 10–50 mm

In wiping the joint, the top edge is cleaned and the solder is drawn up and round from the base. The pressure on the cloth is changed from the sides to the centre, to leave the joint convex at the sides and concave at the angle (Figure 84D). There must be enough solder on the side of the joint to provide a good cover.

Alternative methods of jointing

As an alternative to the ordinary wiped-soldered joint the taft or finger-wiped joint is used. Similar to the finger-wiped joint is the cup-and-cone joint, for which fine solder is used instead of plumber's solder. This joint is generally used for gas pipes. Various mechanical joints have also from time to time been put forward for use as alternatives to the wiped-soldered joint, but none has been used except in a very limited way.

Figure 85   Soldered spigot joint

mouth of pipe chamfered

mouth of pipe opened out

A using cutting tool

B using mandrel

The soldered spigot joint

The soldered spigot joint is formed by inserting a tinned liner into the prepared end of the pipe, shaped to provide a close fit, and bonding the contact area between the liner and the pipe with fine grain solder. The end of the liner may be slightly chamfered and the outer surface of the liner is tinned prior to insertion.

A suitable solder is one conforming to Grade 'A' of BS 219, which covers an alloy containing 65 per cent tin and 35 per cent lead. The amount of solder used on each joint is very small.

The soldered spigot joint is primarily intended for application to all lead connections to brass tail-pieces in distributing pipes. It is also used for running joints and for joints to lead waste pipes up to 40 mm internal diameter. The special tools for making the soldered spigot joint are of a simple type: four coning tools, two cutters, and a

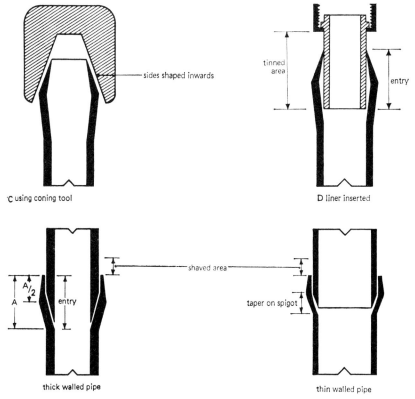

C using coning tool — sides shaped inwards

D liner inserted — tinned area, entry

E preparation for lead-to-lead joints — thick walled pipe (A, A/2, entry), thin walled pipe (shaved area, taper on spigot)

set of steel and boxwood mandrels suffice for all average work with 10- to 40-mm-diameter pipe of usual wall thicknesses. The hollow wood coning tools are made to different tapers so as to accommodate different wall thicknesses of pipe, and it is necessary to check that the right coning tool is selected to give a suitable taper.

The procedure for making the solder spigot joint is as follows:

First operation – the cutting tool is held firmly in a pipe and gently rotated; any attempt to force it may cut too thick a shaving and make the operation a more strenuous one than it need be. The small end of the cutting tool is filled with tallow to stop shavings falling into the pipe. Shavings are cleared from the cutting tool as the operation proceeds. The inside of the pipe is chamfered down to leave a fine edge of 2 mm or less (Figure 85A).

Second operation – the specially shaped steel mandrel is inserted into the chamfered end of the pipe and gently hammered until the pipe is opened to the required depth. The mandrel is smeared with tallow to keep the lead clean. Heat gently applied to thick-walled pipe will greatly assist the opening operations (Figure 85B). The minimum entry for a service or distributing pipe is 32 mm.

Third operation – a hollow hardwood cone is tapped down over the widened pipe end to shape the sides inwards. Ensure that the end of the socket is tapered evenly (Figure 85c).

Fourth operation – the tapering of the pipe end is continued until, when tested, the brass liner can be readily, but not loosely, inserted: before the liner is finally inserted its outside surface is cleaned and tinned and the surplus solder wiped off. As not all brass liners have a perfectly square end, it is an advantage to square off the end with a smooth file and slightly chamfer (Figure 85D).

Final operation – before introducing the brass liner to the pipe, the top edge of the socket should be neatly filed off, or cut with a knife, to a clean square edge. The liner is then inserted and gently tapped home to ensure close contact at the bottom of the joint. The liner may be slightly smeared with non-corrosive flux paste before insertion.

Heat is gently applied to the liner or spigot part of the joint and then with care to the lower half of the socket. The heat is then mainly concentrated on the brass just above the socket. The solder is applied to one side of the joint and, with the heat spread, it will flow into the bonding area of the joint. When a bright ring of solder is formed all round the shoulder of the joint, gently heat the socket with a moving flame until bubbles of flux cease to rise. The solder will remain molten for a short time, and surplus solder can be neatly wiped off for a clean finish.

For thin-walled pipes, waste pipes and traps it is not essential to use a cutter. Open the pipe with a mandrel for entry and clean the internal surface with a knife or shavehook.

For lead-to-lead joints one pipe end is rasped down to a spigot and the other is shaped to a socket as for lead-to-brass joints (Figure 85E). When applying heat to lead-to-lead joints a general heat, not concentrated in any one place, is required. The soldered spigot joint is best made in a vertical position.

Taft or finger-wiped joint

To make this joint the end of the pipe is 'belled' out by driving in a hardwood cone or turn-pin until the liner or spigot pipe end can be accommodated to a depth equal to about half its diameter. The inside of the pipe end is cleaned and fluxed and the outside blacked. The liner or spigot pipe end is prepared as described for ordinary wiped joints. The joint is firmly fixed and plumber's solder applied and wiped (Figure 86).

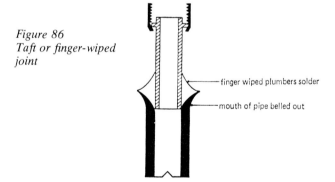

Figure 86
Taft or finger-wiped
joint

finger wiped plumbers solder

mouth of pipe belled out

The cup-and-cone joint is similarly prepared, but fine solder (tinman's) is run into the cup to fill it instead of wiping-in plumber's solder.

17
Roof Weathering

The roofs of homes in this country are usually covered with tiles or slates. Not many new homes have slated roofs because of the very high costs involved. The plumber seldom fixes the roof tiles but he has an important job to do in making the roof watertight.

He is responsible for what is known as the 'weathering', that is, the gutters, aprons and flashings which render watertight those parts of the roof where the tiles abut brickwork or pipes. On a modern house roof weathering presents few problems because of the simplicity of design. In many cases, there is but one chimney pot which terminates the flue of the central heating plant. The parts to be weathered are the chimney stack and the soil and vent pipe where it emerges through the tiles.

Weathering a chimney

No matter how closely fitting the tiles may be to the brickwork where the chimney stack emerges through the roof, they cannot be made watertight without the weatherings. At the back of the chimney there must be a gutter to take away the rainwater as it streams down the roof slope. Down each side of the stack there must be flashings and soakers to keep the driving rain from striking the brickwork and running down into the roof space. The soakers also prevent the discharge from the backgutter from getting through to the roof space, by directing or channelling it towards the roof slope and on its way to the rainwater gutters at the eaves. The front apron protects the face of the chimney stack where it comes through the tiles. Although side flashings with soakers are the most effective method of weathering the sides of the chimney stack, the flashing can continue in one piece from the brickwork on to the tiles. The illustrations show the arrangement of weathering a chimney, which applies no matter what material is used for the weathering.

The work of preparing and fixing roof weathering is a highly skilled job. The householder should see to it that they are done properly by a skilled plumber because a leaking roof can cause serious damage to property. Do not allow the builder to use cement fillets as a substitute for weathering materials.

Where a soil and vent pipe or a flue pipe penetrates the tiles a weathering is made by means of sleeve, or 'slate', as it is usually called by plumbers. Once again it is stressed that a cement fillet is not suitable.

Materials used for roof weathering

Sheet copper, lead, zinc and aluminium are all suitable metals for roof weathering. An asphalt bonded asbestos sheet of laminate construction called Nuralite is now widely used by plumbers. It is highly resistant to atmospheric corrosion and being non-metallic it is not subject to electrolytic decomposition. It is an excellent material for weathering and it costs less than the traditional metals.

The principles adopted in weathering a chimney are the same whatever material is used. The techniques employed in manipulating the materials differ somewhat. For instance sheet lead can be 'bossed' into required shapes by a skilled plumber or it can be cut and welded. Copper can be welded or brazed. Nuralite is manipulated by simple methods and the Nuralite Company Limited, Higham, nr Rochester, Kent, will send an excellent instruction manual to any plumber on application.

Zinc is a traditional metal for roof weathering and it is now produced in convenient 10-m rolls in standard widths of 150, 240, 300, 480, 600 mm. It can be worked quite easily and soldered without difficulty. It has been given a trade name of 'Zincon'. The descriptions of the various roof weathering applications are for Zincon but the general principles are similar for all materials.

The weathering applications are shown in Figures 87 to 94.

Figure 87
Complete stack flashings

Figure 88
A   *Stepped flashing*
     over slates
B   *Backgutter*

back gutter

zincon clips

cover
flashing

soakers

stepped flashing
over slates

stepped
flashing

front apron

Figure 89
Ridge saddle pieces

A

B

cover flashing

soaker

Figure 90
Stepped flashing
over soakers

Figure 91
Soaker detail

front apron

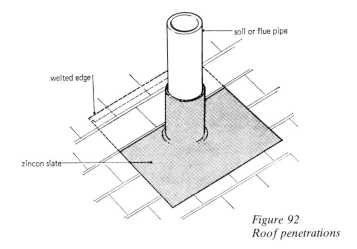

soil or flue pipe

welted edge

zincon slate

Figure 92
Roof penetrations

Figure 93
Cover flashing to felt roof

Figure 94
Valley gutter

zincon clip

welted edge

tile batten

Valley gutter section

section

Stack flashings

The soft malleable temper of Zincon flashing strip makes stack flashing easy as well as economic. Cover flashings, stepped flashings and front aprons are made in the normal way. Backgutters can be cut and soldered together with no weak spots.

Wedges for joints should be cut from the flashing strip and galvanized nails should be used. No treatment to the surface is needed when bedding the material in mortar joints. Where profiled tiles are used, Zincon can usually be formed into the profile of the tile. Allowance should be made for extra material needed to take up this profile in the case of front aprons.

For deeply profiled tiles it is necessary to cut the strip and tuck it into the profile.

Where chimney stack penetrates the roof at a ridge, the side flashings are joined with a saddle piece. This is formed with a lapped and soldered joint.

Side flashings fixed to brickwork are cut with steps, each step being turned into a joint, wedged, and pointed in. The distance between the internal angle of the step and the line of the roof should not be less than 50 mm and, if the roof covering is plain tiles or slates, the side flashing laps over the upstands of soakers coursed in with the tiles or slates. The soakers are folded to turn up at least 75 mm against the side of the stack and to extend 100 to 125 mm under the tiles or slates.

The free edge of the flashing is stiffened with a 25-mm fold. Where the roof covering is single-lap tiling or sheet material the flashing extends on to the roof covering 100 to 125 mm. The free edge is secured with 40-mm-wide Zincon clips spaced at 300-mm centres and nailed to roof timbers.

Where soil vent pipes or flue pipes penetrate roofs, slates can be easily formed to provide the weather-proofing. The slate is cut to course in with the tile or slate module and a short length of pipe soldered in at the appropriate angle. This length of pipe can be cut and soldered from flat strip. This technique need not be limited to pipe sections and can be extended to roof penetrations of any outline. In the case of flat roofs the same technique should be used except that the slate should be laid over the first layer of felt and under the second two layers.

Felt roofing
Zincon can be used as a cover flashing where a felt roof abuts a wall.

Valleys, gutters and ridge tiles
In new work or repairs it is possible to site form Zincon into valleys and ridges to give a long-lasting job with a pleasing appearance. Valley gutters should be formed over timber battens, using a wooden dressing tool. They should be fixed with clips and galvanized nails at 300-mm centres along the edge under the tile or slate. Ridge tiles should also be fixed with clips at 300-mm centres. Overlaps should be 300 mm minimum.

18
Frost Precautions in the Home

This chapter describes how water pipes and other fittings, including cisterns, should be installed in new houses to be safe from damage by freezing. To improve on existing installations, certain recommendations are given and these, although general, should be practicable in most houses.

How to prevent pipes from freezing

Obviously prevention is better than cure and the prevention of frost damage to water pipes is not difficult or expensive. If it is understood from the start that if the house is heated the pipes cannot freeze and that if water pipes outside the house are laid in the ground below the penetration level of frost they will not be affected, it is clear that the cheapest and most effective method of avoiding frost damage is:

(a) Keep the house warm throughout.
(b) Run pipes in protected places wherever possible.
(c) If pipes have to be exposed to cold or draughts see that they are protected by efficient lagging.

It should be understood that lagging a pipe in an exposed place is inferior to fixing the pipe unlagged in a warm area because it does not matter how thick the lagging, it can only give a limited protection against continued hard frost.

All pipes should be fixed with proper falls so they can be emptied of water when a building is left vacant. Where there is a dip in the pipework that cannot be drained then a draintap should be provided at the lowest point.

Why some British plumbing is vulnerable to frost

In most parts of Great Britain the temperature does not fall low enough every winter to give rise to trouble from burst pipes, and we never have long periods of exceptionally low temperature such as occur regularly in Canada or the United States of America. Nevertheless, burst pipes in America are a far less frequent occurrence than in this country, a state of affairs arising only in part from the greater use of central heating throughout that continent, since full central heating is by no means universal in poorer class property. Much of the difference arises from the fact that it is customary to take the rising main up an inside wall (generally that of the central chimney stack) and to place the cold-water storage cistern with one side in contact with the kitchen or sitting-room chimney flue. This precaution does not necessitate appreciably increased installation costs, for it will be seen from Figures 95A and B that the length of supply pipes is similar in both American and English practice. (In Figures 95–99 the heavy arrows indicate the vulnerable area.) Occasionally it is less convenient for branch mains, but with a little ingenuity in designing the pipe layout this can usually be overcome.

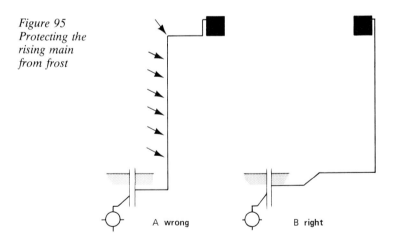

Figure 95
Protecting the
rising main
from frost

A wrong   B right

The only difficulty likely to arise is the branch to the kitchen sink. In houses with suspended wooden ground floors, the 15-mm branch from the main may be run in the void beneath the floor to the sink unit, but care must be taken to lag all pipework in this void to protect it from the through draught from the air bricks at the front and back of the building. Do not, under any circumstances, block the air bricks: through ventilation is essential to prevent musty smells in ground-floor rooms and, worse, dry rot.

A drain-off cock must be fitted in an accessible position.

In many properties the ground floors are solid concrete and the water main enters the building through a pipe duct. As access is not possible under the slab, the supply to the kitchen sink should be taken through the first-floor void and brought down, if possible, on an internal wall surface adjacent to the sink.

While it is advocated that cold-water supply pipes should be routed through warm areas wherever possible, care must be taken to ensure that the water is not actually heated. Indeed, cold-water pipes in any warm area should be lagged to prevent condensation.

Where hot- and cold-water pipes are run in pairs horizontally, one above the other, especially on the surface of walls, always ensure that the cold-water pipe is beneath the hot-water pipe and separated by at least 50 mm (preferably 75 mm) to prevent condensation.

Why pipes burst

A study of the action of ice formation which leads to burst pipes suggests other ways in which damage may be obviated. The formation of ice in a water pipe rarely takes place simultaneously throughout its length, but proceeds progressively from the coldest point towards the warmer points. As is well known, when water freezes its volume increases approximately 9 per cent. If a pipe has one end open and unobstructed, and if ice formation begins at the closed end, it is possible for freezing to continue steadily towards the open end without increasing the pressure on the walls of the pipe, (Figure 97A). Indeed, such a pipe may be repeatedly frozen solid in this way without the slightest risk of fracture. If, however, the freezing begins at the open end (see Figure 97B) a plug is formed, and as the water cools towards the closed end, pressure is built up until after repeated freezings a burst is inevitable, no matter what thickness of material is used for the walls of the pipe.

In the case of the normal domestic service pipe, the main in the street practically never freezes and so acts as the open end or relief valve, provided always that freezing starts at the remote end. If, however, freezing starts at some intermediate point, and there forms a plug of ice, trouble is likely to be serious between that point and the house end of the pipe. For this reason particular care should

Figure 96
The position of the
cold supply to the
sink

A right

B wrong

cold
wall

cold
wall

ice plug

Figure 97
Cause of frost
burst   A   B

be taken where it enters the house. It is generally considered in this country that a pipe buried 0.760 m deep in ordinary streets or garden ground is below the limit of frost action, even in severe weather. Again, in the case of a pipe passing over a series of windows or into and out of buildings, there is more than one point likely to freeze and form a plug at a comparatively early stage. In all such cases relatively high pressures will be built up as freezing proceeds from the plug towards the dead end of the pipe and sooner or later a burst will occur.

A pipe buried in an external wall is more likely to freeze than one fixed on the internal surface of that wall since, apart from other reasons, there will be less thickness of wall to protect it. Naturally, too, if it should burst, the damage done to the structure and the cost of repair will be greater.

Pipes which are exposed to cold draughts tend to lose heat rapidly and thus run an increased risk of freezing. Thus, pipes in roof spaces can be protected to a considerable extent simply by covering them with any material which will protect them from draught. Actually, the most vulnerable position for a pipe in a house of normal type occurs at the point where it is carried up the outer wall and passes unprotected close to an open eave, where it is exposed to continual draughts (Figure 98).

Figure 98
Exposure at eaves

Insulation

There are on the market at the moment a great variety of insulating materials, most of which are satisfactory for their purpose. It should be remembered, however, that even the best insulating material must allow for some heat loss, and that during prolonged spells of cold weather it is only a matter of time before the temperature of the pipe falls to a dangerous limit, unless, of course, fresh warmer water is passed through it from time to time. For this reason, therefore, a pipe placed in a wholly exposed position, even after insulation with the best possible material, is not so safe as an uninsulated pipe placed in a room or against a chimney the temperature of which never falls to freezing point for appreciable periods. Of course, it cannot be guaranteed that the house will not from time to time be left uninhabited, but when this is the case, precautions can and should be taken to see that the pipes are emptied. The boxing-in of pipes in a properly insulated chase generally gives more protection than casual insulation wrapped round the pipe.

Pipes in exposed positions

Particular care should be taken when the pipes are placed in exposed positions and protected in insulation to see that all points in the length of the pipe are equally and fully protected, for any part less protected than the rest provides a point at which a plug of ice may form. If freezing continues and a volume of water is entrapped between the pipe and a closed end or even another ice plug, increased pressure must occur and there is a risk of bursting.

Protecting the cold-water cistern

The means commonly taken to protect the cold-water storage tank show many examples of wrongly applied insulation. It is common for such cisterns to be protected with an ordinary boarded casing filled with sawdust or some better insulator, but with the feed pipe far less adequately lagged (Figure 99a). Even if the cistern were to freeze solid, which would take a long time, there would probably be no actual splitting of the metal. The small volume of water in the feed pipe will, however, not only tend to freeze more quickly, but after several freezings will almost certainly burst the pipe. This, therefore, needs more and not less careful protection than the tank.

Perhaps the commonest mistake where cisterns are thoughtlessly protected is to box-in the feed pipes in the same casing. To some extent, of course, the volume of water in the cistern tends to keep the feed warm, but it will be seen from Figure 99b that in most cases the amount of effective insulation for the pipe is less than one half that which it has been thought necessary to provide for the cistern. Either the pipe should be separately treated (Figure 99c) or else an extra space in the boxing of the cistern should be allowed on the pipe side.

Again, it is very common to cut through the casing for a feed pipe without any precautions being taken to insulate the pipe where it passes through the boards or sheeting (Figure 99D). Such an open hole through the casing and round the pipe may also permit the passage of a considerable draught. This is a very undesirable condition, because, as has been said before, cold air in movement is much more dangerous than air that is completely stationary, which, by the way, is one of the best possible insulating media.

Figure 99 Insulating the cistern

Where any form of organic insulation has been used and trouble is experienced with mice or rats, some protection can be given by wrapping the outside of the insulating materials with thin bitumen felt. It is not an absolute safeguard, but appears to be distasteful to most rodents. Moreover, it reduces the passage of air through the insulating material, and prevents accidental wetting, thus giving increased efficiency.

A further point in connection with the use of makeshift insulating materials is in connection with the covering of external waste pipes, particularly from baths and lavatory basins. It is quite common in the country to see such wastes covered with a sack, perhaps straw filled, nailed to the wall above and beneath. When dry this may give some protection. When wet, it is probably worse than useless as the pipe will be surrounded by actual ice, but be effectively shut off from the warmth of the sun in the middle of the day. All insulation must be kept absolutely dry, preferably by boxing-in with a carefully jointed waterproof casing. If this is impossible, then wrapping with waterproof felt will help.

However perfect the insulating material, it is practically valueless when wet, and even when only damp suffers a considerable loss of efficiency.

Thawing out
Where through lack of protection lead pipes have been frozen, care is necessary in thawing them out. Even if a burst has not occurred at once because the expansion on cooling has been accommodated by the stretching or give of the pipe, it is quite possible for the trouble to arise later from careless thawing. The warming should be done slowly, starting at the open end of the pipe so that increased pressures are automatically relieved.

Hints to the householder

It is essential that you should be familiar with your plumbing system, particularly the hot- and cold-water services. A study of the chapters on these services in this book should enable the householder to cope with an emergency, but if there is any doubt about the draining of the system or if it is safe to use the boiler, then the advice of a qualified plumber should be sought.

The golden rules at all times are:
1 Find out where the stopvalve is located.
2 See that it will shut off the main supply.
3 Locate and label any other stopvalves in the house.
4 Repair all leaking taps.

5 Check up on the ball valves of the w.c. cistern and storage cistern
   in the roof. See that they are not leaking and that they work
   properly. It will be as well to ensure that the overflow pipes from
   the cistern are not obstructed.

When there is a likelihood of a severe frost lasting some days:

Adequate precautions depend upon individual circumstances. If,
for example, your house is warmed by central heating, your pipes
routed on internal walls and properly lagged in any danger areas,
then you have taken all the precautions necessary.

If, on the other hand, you have no general heating and there are
very cold spots in the house, then it is advisable to turn off and drain
the cold-water rising main, which is simple enough to do. More
difficult are the other services, such as the cold feed and cold-water
down service from the cold-water storage cistern. It is impracticable
to drain the entire system every night, quite apart from wasting
water – and possibly dangerous if you use a boiler and forget to turn
on the cold-feed valve.

This is a problem particularly affecting elderly people living in
older-type properties, who cannot afford to install a heating system
or, even if the system is installed, cannot afford the fuel to run it.
Anybody in this situation should consult their local town hall for
guidance and possible financial assistance.

If a pipe in the house freezes:

1 Shut off the main stopvalve – or if it is controlled by an adjacent
   stopvalve, shut that off. If the pipe is a distributing pipe from the
   storage cistern and is not controlled by a valve, inspect it first to
   see that it has not burst before attempting to thaw it out.
2 Try to thaw the pipe by using cloths soaked in hot water or safe
   portable heaters. A blowlamp may be used if the householder is
   accustomed to its operation. Always start thawing at the nearest
   open tap on the pipe and work away from it.

If a pipe bursts:

1 If the burst is discovered before the thaw begins shut off the main
   stopvalve; this will stop flooding if the burst is on the main pipe. If
   the burst is on a distributing pipe from the cistern, close the
   control stopvalve if there is one. Otherwise open all the cold-

water taps being fed from the cistern to drain it off as quickly as possible. The main stopvalve must be closed, of course, to cut off the feed.

2 Call in a qualified plumber as soon as possible.

The hot-water system in frosty weather

Many householders get worried in freezing weather about the hot-water system of the house, particularly if it is an installation with a boiler. They have heard of boiler explosions in other people's houses. There is little cause for alarm, however, providing normal precautions are taken. In fact it is advisable to keep the hot-water system working in frosty weather because the fire – and the pipes – can give that essential background warmth which might well prevent the plumbing becoming frozen.

The essential thing is that the system is full of water and that none of the pipes is frozen.

If the cold feed to the hot-water cylinder is blocked by ice *do not light the boiler*.

If it is already lit, the first signs of trouble will be no water at hot-water taps, but there is no immediate danger if your boiler is controlled by a thermostat.

The greatest danger is from an open fire with a back boiler which has no heat control system. If this fire is burning, it can rapidly boil the water out of the cylinder. At best, the cylinder will collapse under excessive external pressure. At worst, the cold feed may thaw, allowing cold water into a red-hot boiler jacket – which is likely to explode. There are, however, early warning signs: loud banging from the hot-water cylinder and hot water discharging from the cold-water tank overflow. If this happens, put out the fire immediately and let the system cool. Do not interfere with anything. Call a plumber without delay.

It is not advisable for the householder to drain his hot-water system without expert advice. Unfortunately, it is not possible to give any general instructions about draining systems, because many have been installed by incompetent persons and an inspection would be necessary before a decision could be made – even by an expert.

If the water from a copper hot-water storage cylinder was drained when the vent pipe was frozen, the cold feedvalve closed, and the taps at the fitments closed, the cylinder might well collapse like a tin can crushed by a heavy boot. A partial vacuum is caused in the cylinder. When this reduction in internal pressure takes place, the external atmospheric pressure is such that the material from which the cylinder is constructed is not sufficiently strong to withstand the enormous external pressure exerted on the cylinder, with the result that the body of the cylinder is crushed in – or more simply, the cylinder collapses.

19
Water Softening in the Home

As rain sinks into the ground it begins to dissolve some of the minerals in the earth, so that when water comes from a spring or from a well – depending to a large extent upon the nature of earth through which it passed originally – it can have dissolved in it a good many different things.

Generally speaking, water that has gone through chalky soils is hard while that which has gone through sandy soils is likely to be soft.

It is the presence of calcium and magnesium elements in water that hardens it and prevents lather being formed easily. The fat in the soap acts upon these calcium and magnesium elements – upon the hardness – and combines to form an insoluble scum of white curds that float on the water. Put soap in hard water and after a few rubs the water is milky in colour. It gets milkier according to the amount of hardness in the water and number of rubs you give the soap until soap scum – decomposed soap or greasy curdled fat – forms. A lather forms when, and only when, the hardness has been neutralized, but the hardness is still in the water.

This scum, because of its sticky nature, clogs the pores of the skin, mats the hair, clings to and discolours clothes and fabrics washed in it and sticks to dishes, silverware and glass. It sticks round wash-basins, kitchen bowls, kitchen sinks and baths.

There are two forms of hardness in water – temporary and permanent. It is necessary to explain the term temporary.

When hard water is heated, some of the hardness is thrown down and evidence of this can be seen in the domestic kettles of homes in hard-water areas. That 'fur', or 'scale', is temporary hardness. There are minerals that cannot be removed in this way and substances left dissolved in the water, even after boiling, cause what is called 'permanent' hardness.

When a kettle or a boiler becomes coated with this 'fur', or 'scale', which is a very bad conductor of heat, the water takes longer to boil or requires a great deal more fuel to boil.

Just as 'fur' forms in kettles so it will form around an immersion heater in a hot-water tank, in a back-fire boiler or in the more conventional free-standing boiler whether gas fired, oil fired, or solid-fuel fired. So also, will it form in the coils of a water heater.

If the hardness is allowed to continue depositing, the immersion heater may well burn itself out or if a complaint is made that the heater has lost efficiency and so has to be removed for descaling, it may well be found that the extent of the scale formation is such that the heater cannot be withdrawn from the tank through the hole originally cut for it, which may well mean the replacement of the hot-water tank.

The first sign of trouble is often a complaint from one of the family that the water does not get as hot as it used to or not as quickly as it did. How can it when more and more scale has to be heated before the water. itself is heated? In boilers and hot-water pipes the scale can thicken and thicken until it chokes off the flow of water and cleaning by a chemical process or complete replacement becomes necessary – an expensive business.

Hard water wastes time, soap and fuel, causes hard work and can in certain circumstances impair health.

The benefits of soft water

Softened water saves soap because only a touch of soap is needed to produce ample lather.

It preserves beauty because it keeps skin soft and supple, as nature intended, keeps pores clean and free, allowing the skin to breathe and improves complexion by eliminating hard-water blemishes and prevents 'dishpan hands'.

Softened water improves home laundering because it washes clothes soft and clean, and it is essential for obtaining perfect results with washing machines. It simplifies washing up because it quickly removes grease, and the dishes can be drained clean without wiping. Glassware and silver drain dry to a high polish.

If softened water is used the burden of housework is eased because floors, woodwork, tiles, baths and sinks are quickly cleaned without hard scouring.

Softened water saves tea and coffee because less tea and coffee are needed to obtain the true full flavour and colour.

Plumbing repairs are reduced by soft water because there is no 'scale' to choke the flow in boilers, pipes and radiators – even in car radiators – while heated coils last their full life.

The water softener

By passing hard water through a water softener, hardness-free water can be obtained. The water from one tap can be softened by using a small portable unit, but for household purposes the ideal unit is one which is connected into the cold main-water supply pipe so that all water passes through the softener, and emerges as hardness-free water from every tap in the house.

A water softener is simple to install and maintain and once the softening material in the equipment becomes saturated with hardness, all that needs to be done to bring it back into its original efficiency is to pass ordinary common salt through it. In some models the salt is poured into the container in its ordinary dry form while in the other models – the semi-automatic and the automatic models – the salt is introduced as a brine solution. In either case the salt is rinsed through the softener and once all the salt has gone down the drain the water softener is again ready to give its rated output of hardness-free water. This process is known as regeneration and so long as the water softener is regularly regenerated it will for many years give thoroughly satisfactory service.

The size and type of unit required depends on the degree of hardness of the water requiring to be softened, the number of people using water – for this determines the amount used – and, of course, the space available for the positioning of the unit. They are installed in kitchens, in cloakrooms, in larders, in cupboards under stairs, in garages – in fact in any reasonably accessible position where regeneration can be carried out without difficulty and where easy access can be obtained to water main and drain.

The water-softening process

For years household water softening has been undertaken by what is known as the Base Exchange process. The process is virtually the same today, but is becoming more widely referred to as the Ion Exchange method of softening.

A number of ion exchangers are produced in this country. One, a unifunctional polystyrene resin, is known as Zeo-Karb 225. These ion exchangers have replaced the earlier natural greensand and synthetic materials but the principle of operation remains the same.

Zeo-Karb 225 in its sodium form is used for water softening. A quantity of this material, which is of a golden brown colour and spheroid in shape, is filled into a container and hard water passes through it – generally in a downward direction. The softening material has the unique property of changing its sodium content for the hardness content in the water. In other words, the calcium and magnesium hardness-forming elements in the water are changed into their equivalent sodium elements – nothing more – so that the water contains exactly the same quantity of elements as originally but in another form – in a sodium form. Household water softening is in fact just as simple as that.

Hard water is passed through the resin until it is saturated with calcium and magnesium – saturated with hardness – whereupon the water coming out of the container will be as hard as that going in. The resin is exhausted but as a proof of the further simplicity of household water softening the resin can be brought back to its original condition – to its full water-softening power – by a process known as 'regeneration'.

Sodium must be put back into the resin and what easier way than by passing ordinary common salt – sodium chloride – through it.

Exactly the reverse action to that described takes place. The calcium and magnesium hardness-forming elements are thrown out of the resin which takes up sodium from the salt. The hardness in chloride form is washed down the drain.

Water-softening equipment

The portable unit

The most simple form of household water softener is the portable unit available from good plumbers' merchants and from Permutit Ltd. This is a hard plastics container with polythene handle cap, inlet bend, and outlet spout. A rubber hose is attached to the inlet bend and a rubber connection is pushed on to the tap from which water is drawn. It can be hot water or cold for neither the resinous softening material nor the hard polythene is affected by water temperature.

The softener is delivered already filled with the resin, so that having attached the hose the tap can be turned on. Water enters through the bend on the side of the container and is spread over the resin by means of a distributor pipe. The hard water passes downward through the resin, the exchange previously described takes place and hardness-free water is collected in a pipe at the bottom of the container and passes from the outlet spout under pressure. Turn off the tap and the flow stops.

The quantity of resin in the unit shown is capable of producing 680 litres of hardness-free water providing the hardness of the water is 16°. If there is more hardness in each litre of the water the number of litres softened will be less and, of course, if there is less hardness the number of litres softened will be more.

When the resin is exhausted – or saturated with hardness – the user removes the handle cap and pours into the container 0.50 kg of salt – ordinary common salt – replaces the handle cap and turns on the tap so that the salt dissolves and rinses through the resin until this is regenerated and returned to its original condition.

The manufacturers supply with this unit – and, in fact, with each of their household water softeners – a small simple testing outfit consisting of a shake bottle marked at 40 cc and a bottle of soap solution with a dripper top. With this it is possible to check if softened water is being obtained, that regeneration needs to be carried out or that all salt has been rinsed off. In other words, that regeneration has been completed.

Mains-supply unit

The portable appliance is an extremely convenient unit for carrying round but the ideal water softener for the household is a mains-supply unit designed for connecting to the main water supply. In general, the principle of the mains-supply water softener is the same as for the portable unit already described but there are what is known to the manufacturers as dry-salting and wet-salting units.

In recent years the near-monopoly of one company in the supply of mains-supply water softeners for domestic use has ended, and there is now a wide selection of models from UK manufacturers as well as imported models, many at competitive prices. Today most have rust-proof plastic or fibreglass cases and more sophisticated controls. One has an excellent device which senses when regeneration is required. This over-rides the timing clock, so that when little water has been used in the household, needless regeneration is avoided, thus saving the cost of salt.

Assessing water requirements

A water softener must be considered against the requirements of the particular household. It is advisable to assess the likely consumption of water, which obviously depends upon the number of persons in residence. In a household where a check was made by a water meter it was discovered that the average consumption of water per person per day, over quite a long period, was 159 litres. This was water for every use and in that particular household nothing but softened water was obtainable. The meter was used not only to check water consumption but also to check the efficiency of the water softener installed. There is good reason to believe this is a fair average consumption of water per person per day, but of course there are households in which the average consumption is higher than this and some where it is lower and it is reasonable to work on this basis. Having ascertained the number of people in residence and multiplied this by 159, it is recommended that the figure should be multiplied again by 8 in order to ascertain the weekly consumption of water in litres. Having arrived at this figure and with the knowledge of the hardness of the water as supplied to the residence, it is possible to determine with reasonable accuracy the size of water softener which is capable of producing at least one week's supply of softened water between each regeneration. A water softener of this size is recommended by the manufacturers, for after long experience they have reached the conclusion that, in the case of manually regenerated water softeners, it is better that regeneration should be undertaken at regular intervals rather than at more frequent intervals. It is better to install a water softener capable of softening more than one week's normal requirements for this then takes into account the possibility of guests or visitors who will, if staying for any period of time, increase the consumption of water. There is no doubt a great deal of harm has been done to the cause of water softening by the installation of units which are quite incapable of producing water in quantity to meet the needs of a household.

Connecting the softener

To connect these mains-supply water softeners, it is necessary to break into the cold main-water inlet pipe and run a hard-water inlet feed to the water softener and bring a return pipe from the water softener to the supply pipe and fit between these two connections a valve which becomes known as the by-pass valve, which is closed when the water softener is in operation. It is recommended that a valve be fitted on both the hard-water inlet and soft-water outlet lines for emergency purposes and to enable the owner of the equipment to isolate the water softener.

Most water companies insist upon the fitting of a non-return valve before the water softener. A waste pipe is required to take the effluent during regeneration away to an outside gully or drain and the size of this waste pipe should be determined by the size of the hard-water inlet pipe and, of course, the length of the run of the waste and whether or not it contains a number of bends and elbows.

20
Flushing Cisterns Explained

A fixed quantity of water must be discharged to cleanse water closets and for this purpose flushing cisterns are used. A cistern is stipulated for the following reasons:

1 To provide sufficient water to flush and cleanse the pan effectively and reseal the trap with fresh water.
2 To prevent waste of water by using a regulated volume to each flushing.
3 To break direct contact between the water supply and the fixture so that, should a stoppage occur in the fixture, the pollution of the water supply by foul water being siphoned back into the main will be prevented.

The flushing cistern generally used is known as a valveless, waste water preventing, siphonic cistern, so called because there is no valve through which water from the cistern can run to waste down the flush pipe and because the discharge of water is due to siphonic action. Although flushing cisterns differ in design and construction, most of them depend upon the principle of siphonage for the discharge of their contents. The cistern has provision made for the supply of water through an automatic ball valve situated either on the right-hand or left-hand side. On the opposite side, provision is made for the connection of an overflow pipe which allows excess water to discharge where it will be noticed, but will not cause a nuisance or damage property. The flush pipe connection is at the bottom of the cistern.

It is only necessary in this description of flushing cisterns to deal with two types: (1) a straight outlet cistern and (2) a low-level cistern, both of which are in common use in normal houses.

Straight outlet cistern

Construction

This type of cistern has the working parts contained in a cast iron vessel, with a cylindrical well in the centre of the bottom. In this well is a vertical outlet pipe with a lip at the weir and an enlargement near the bottom, to assist in the setting up of siphonage. The outlet pipe weir terminates slightly above the normal overflow weir of the cistern.

A heavy cast-iron bell of conical shape, flared out at the bottom, fits over the outlet pipe and stands in the well. It has a diameter at the base which allows it to move up and down freely in the well, but has only a small space between it and the wall of the well.

The bell has a loop at the top to which is attached a lever and a chain, and near the bottom is a small air-break hole. Projecting lugs leave a clear space between the bottom of the bell and the bottom of the cistern.

In this type of cistern, as shown in Figure 100, a simple inverted U-tube is formed, the short leg being the annular space between the outlet pipe and the inside of the bell, and the long leg being the outlet pipe and its continuation as a flush pipe.

Water is supplied through an automatic ball valve which should be adjusted to shut off when the water level is about 25 mm below the overflow weir of the tank.

Action

Figure 100A shows the cistern ready for discharge, the bell in its normal position and the automatic ball valve shut off, the water level being the same under the bell as in the cistern. Air which previously filled the space between the bell and outlet pipe has now been expelled through the outlet pipe as the water has risen. The bell is raised by the lever and chain (B), but actual siphonage is not set up until the bell is lowered.

On release of the chain the bell, owing to its weight, drops heavily on the water beneath it, which cannot escape quickly enough through the small space between the bell and the vertical wall of the well. It is compelled to rise inside the bell and flows over the outlet weir and down the long leg of the U-tube, thus setting up siphonic action, as shown in (C). This siphonic action will continue until the level of water is reduced to the air hole in the bell, as shown in (D), when an admission of air breaks the siphon and allows the cistern to fill again.

Figure 100
Flushing cistern
action

weir

air break hole

bell

well

outlet pipe

A

B

C

D

Low-level cistern

A low-level cistern is generally part of a suite, consisting of cistern, flush pipe and pan, designed for the efficient working of each part and a relatively silent flush.

Construction

The vessel of the low-level cistern, as shown in Figure 101, is of heavy glazed pottery ware. Although it contains the usual quantity of water it has a comparatively small width, thus taking up a minimum of space. An inverted U-tube is formed in the cistern, a straight 45-mm-diameter pipe and the flush pipe forming the long leg.

The short leg is formed by the inlet pipe in the cistern near the bottom. There is no bell in this cistern, but the balanced plunger is fixed inside the inlet to the U-tube and rests on a rubber-coated rod.

The plunger is connected by levers to a small turn handle fixed on the outside of the cistern. All these parts are made of heavily galvanized iron to prevent the formation of rust.

Connected to the crown of the U-tube is a small brass air pipe which terminates about three inches from the bottom of the cistern. Its function is to admit air to stop the siphonic action at the conclusion of the flush. The weir of the U-tube is situated above the overflow weir of the cistern, and in this regard a similarity to the straight outlet type of cistern will be observed.

As the height at which the cistern is fixed has a direct bearing on the proper flushing of the pan, it is important that the length of the flush pipe should not be altered by the plumber when fixing the suite. The loss of head of water by fixing the cistern at a low level is offset by the increased diameter of the flush pipe.

Water is supplied through an automatic ball valve which should be adjusted to shut off when the water is about 25 mm below the overflow weir.

Action

As the long leg of the U-tube is open to the atmosphere the water flowing into the cistern will rise in the short leg of the U-tube to the same level as that in the cistern, as shown in Figure 101.

Siphonage is set up by turning the handle on the outside of the cistern. The balanced plunger is thrown upwards, causing a wave motion of the water in the U-tube, as shown at (B).

Figure 101   The low-level cistern

This results in a quantity of water being forced over the weir of the inverted U-tube, and down the long leg causing siphonic action to be set up, such action continuing as shown at (c).

When the level of water in the cistern has been reduced to the inlet of the air-breaking tube, an admittance of air breaks the siphon, as shown at (D).

Owing to the plunger being balanced, it will remain in an upward position during the time the water is discharging from the cistern. As the discharge finishes, it will slowly come to rest on the rubber-coated rod, in its original position.

Dual-flush cistern

A recent development is the dual-flush cistern, designed to save water on what is the highest-usage domestic fitting. This device gives the user a choice of either a 4.5-litre flush or a 9-litre flush.

Figure 102

B *part section of siphon for dual flush cistern*

Figure 102 shows at (A) a typical low-level cistern with a direct-lift piston which raises water within the bell over the inverted U-pipe to create the siphonic action to empty the cistern via the flush pipe into the w.c. pan. The siphon is broken when the water level in the cistern falls to the bottom of the siphon and air is admitted to the chamber.

Figure 102 illustrates at (B) the dual-flush adaptation. For a 4.5-litre discharge the handle is depressed and immediately released. When the water level falls to the top of the siphon, air is admitted to the bell through the air inlet and breaks the action. For a 9-litre flush the handle is held down, causing the rubber washer on the piston to be held hard against the seating, making an airtight seal and preventing the premature entry of air. The siphonic action is then broken either when the water level reaches the bottom of the bell or when the handle is released, allowing the washer to drop away from the seating.

21

Fault Finding, Repairs and Maintenance

Faults in ball valves

Cause	Remedy
Rubber washer worn or defective.	Renew rubber washer.
A piece of rust or other foreign matter on the rubber washer, preventing the washer from fitting correctly on its seat.	Remove the foreign matter or Rewasher the valve.
Ball waterlogged, and instead of floating on the surface of the water remains partly or completely submerged; therefore there is not sufficient power to lever the rubber washer to its seat.	The ball must be drained of water and repaired where defective or Renew the ball.
Ball detached from lever. Incorrect adjustment of the lever.	Re-attach ball to the lever. The lever arm should be bent down at the ball end so that the rubber washer is forced to its seating when the water level is lowered.
Jamming of the ball on some portion of the cistern.	Free the ball and adjust the lever arm to prevent recurrence of the trouble.
The seating of the valve defective and not providing a proper surface for the rubber washer.	Seat of valve may be re-faced or The body of the valve or the complete ball valve replaced.

| Striking arm of the lever in the plunger worn. | File where bearing or Renew lever arm. |

Re-washering a ball valve

1 Shut off water supply at the stop tap.
2 Disconnect the union nut between supply pipe and ballcock.
3 Unscrew the lock nut and remove ballcock from cistern. Should the ballcock have a cap piece, as shown in Figure 103, it is unnecessary to remove the ballcock from the cistern as the cap and split-pin may be removed without removing the complete ball valve.
4 Remove the split-pin to release the lever arm and plunger.
5 Disconnect the extension and valve seating from the body, by using a pipe wrench or spanner on the hexagonal shoulder and holding against the pressure with a rod placed in the water outlet.
6 Take the plunger apart by inserting a flat tool in the lever arm slot, and unscrew the cap piece with pliers or a small wrench.
7 Remove the old rubber washer and clean away any rubber adhering to the cap piece or plunger.
8 Cut a piece of rubber to size and insert it in the plunger cap piece. When a washer is to be cut, place the cap piece on the rubber and give it a light tap. This will mark the correct outline of the circle to be cut. Cut the rubber neatly with the wet blade of a knife and then insert in the plunger cap piece.
9 Screw the cap piece on the plunger and tighten. The rubber washer may have a very slightly convex facing to the seat, as shown in Figure 103. If the washer is too thick, or cut too large, the facing will be too convex (B) and the washer will not last long.
10 File any tool marks off the plunger and place it in the body.
11 Insert the lever arm in the plunger slot, and secure the plunger and lever arms by replacing the split-pin and opening its ends.
12 Screw the extension and valve seat tightly to the body.
13 Replace the ballcock in the cistern.
14 Tighten the lock nut and connect the union nut on the service pipe.
15 Turn on the water supply.

Figure 103
Re-washering a ball valve

The BRS ball valve showing working parts

The ball valve illustrated in Figure 104 was designed by the Department of Scientific and Industrial Research (Building Research Station) to fulfil the urgent need for fittings which would give longer, reliable service, and not be prone to the well known weaknesses of earlier types. We refer, of course, to the corrosion or erosion of the metal seatings which results in the familiar 'saw-cut' effect, and to the sticking of the piston of Portsmouth type valves in certain waters. These disadvantages have been fully overcome, and in the latest design several other most desirable features have been included.

The main features of the BRS ball valve are as illustrated, a nylon nozzle shaped to overcome cavitation and a rubber diaphragm which stops the flow of water when pressed against the nozzle by a plunger. This design ensures that the moving parts of the valve are out of water and therefore free from corrosion and incrustation. The movement of the plunger is controlled by the usual float on a hinged arm, which at its free end is bent down at a right-angle. By means of a thumbscrew, the float can be fixed on this part of the arm at any height depending on the water level required in the cistern. It can also be adjusted radially to avoid any obstacle.

plunger

rubber diaphragm

adjustment screw for float

Figure 104
The BRS ball valve
illustrated above is
manufactured by the
Kings Langley
Engineering Co. Ltd.

cross section
showing nylon nozzle
and working parts assembled

Renewing a tap washer

Step by step

1 Turn off the supply to the tap at the stopvalve.
2 Open the tap to its fullest extent and unscrew the easy-clean shield to expose the hexagon on the headpart (Figure 105A).
3 Using a spanner unscrew the headpart from the body of the tap. The body of the tap should be firmly held with the free hand against the pressure exerted by the spanner.
4 Release the worn washer by removing the nut holding the washer to the jumper (Figure 105B).
5 Replace the washer making sure that it is the correct size for the tap jumper, and tighten the retaining nut.

Figure 105
The bib-tap

grub screw for
fixing crosstop

spindle

gland nut

head

gland packing

gland washers
(two)

joint washers

jumper

seating washer

washer seat

nut

body

A

B

C

6 Replace the headpart and tighten with spanner, again holding the free hand on the tap against the pressure exerted by the spanner. Make certain that the spindle of the tap is still in the open position, otherwise the washer will engage the seating of the tap and prevent the headpart being screwed tightly on the body.

7 Restore the water supply by opening the stopvalve.

Repacking the gland

Step by step

1 Remove the grub screw securing the crosstop (see Figure 105c) and turn the tap fully on to expose as much of the spindle as possible.

2 Unscrew the easy-clean shield and raise it to expose the hexagon head of the tap.

3 Insert a piece of wood or two spring type clothes pegs (Figure 105c) to keep the shield in the raised position. Close the tap and the crosstop will be removed by the upward pressure of the easy-clean shield.

4 Unscrew the gland nut, remove the top washer and pick out the defective gland packing.

5 Re-pack the gland with lamp cotton into which vaseline has been worked. Make two or three turns of the cotton around the spindle in a clockwise direction, pressing it down into the gland box.

6 Replace the top washer and screw down the gland nut firmly.

7 Before replacing the easy-clean cover slip on the crosshead and turn on the tap to ensure that the packing is effective. If it leaks a little, take another turn on the nut.

Faults in screw-down taps

Defect	Cause	Remedy
Water flowing or dripping from the tap outlet when shut hard down.	Worn or defective washer. Piece of grit, rust or other foreign matter on the washer. Defective seat of tap.	Re-washer tap. Remove foreign matter or Re-washer tap. Renew tap.
Water flowing from around spindle or stuffing box screw.	Defective packing in stuffing box. Screw of stuffing box not screwed down tightly.	Renew packing with greased hemp. Tighten stuffing box screw.
Spindle continually slipping when turned and tap will not shut off.	Spindle thread stripped or badly worn.	Renew tap. Renew packing with greased hemp.
Tap hard to turn on and off.	Stuffing box packing too tight. Spindle bent.	Work tallow into stuffing box. Renew tap.
Loud noise in the tap when turned on.	Valve loose on the spindle. Washer loose on valve.	Solder the valve to the spindle or Renew tap. Renew the valve or washer or Renew tap.
Sudden cessation of the flow of water.	Foreign object caught in the stopcock ferrule, stop tap, or a particular tap.	Shut off water and clean out the obstruction.
Stain from water on sanitary fitment.	Stain from leather washer on valve.	Replace leather washer with a fibre washer.

Care of chromium plated fittings

Water fittings are usually made from brass, an alloy of 60–65 per cent copper and 35–40 per cent zinc. The component parts are either made from brass rod, brass tube, brass castings or brass forgings. After all the machining operations are carried out the surface is usually ground and polished. Although brass-polished fittings look pleasant this metal tends to tarnish very quickly. In consequence good-quality water fittings are nickel-plated, which is comparable with a good priming or undercoat and subsequently chromium-plated, which is the top high-gloss finishing coat.

Chrome is extremely hard and resistant to most acids. All that is necessary is to wipe the fittings dry immediately after use and if this is done regularly, fittings will last a lifetime.

Many cleaning materials contain abrasives and it stands to reason that frequent use of these will gradually destroy the protective coating and the life of a chromium-plated water fitting.

Fitting a waste outlet to bath, sink or washbasin

The method of performing this operation is as follows:

1 Remove the lock nut from the thread, and fit a plastics washer over the thread (Figure 106A).
2 Paint the outside of the plug and washer, and around the inside and outside of the outlet hole of the fixture, with white lead paint.
3 Fill the flange of the plug with a mixture of white lead (or white lead oil) and linseed oil putty, and, with a few strands of hemp wound around, insert through the outlet hole (Figure 106B).
4 Paint the washer, and with a little of the putty mixture on it place it over the thread of the plug, and tighten firmly with the lock nut (Figure 106c). When fitting a plug and washer to a fixture with an overflow, a grummet of hemp should be placed between the sink and the washer to prevent the putty mixture being squeezed into the overflow holes of the plug and washer.
5 Adjust the grating bars to a neat finish and clean off surplus putty and paint.

Stoppages in waste pipes

Stoppages in waste pipes are indicated first by a slowing down of the usual rate of discharge of waste water, and finally by a complete stoppage of the discharge. The position of a stoppage may be at any point between the fixture and the point of discharge to the drain, and is caused generally by a gradual silting up of the pipes with matter carried by the waste water. A stoppage usually occurs at fittings, particularly when the burr has not been removed from the pipe after cutting, and also in long runs of pipe with insufficient fall. If effective gratings are fitted on fixture outlets, stoppages caused by foreign objects in the pipes are rare. If foreign objects do pass the fixture grating, they will generally be found in the fixture trap. The trap may be cleaned by removing the cleaning screw (Figure 107).

In modern plumbing systems the trap beneath the kitchen sink and washbasin in the bathroom will often be of the type that can be dismantled without difficulty. This enables the U part of the trap to be cleansed and also allows access to the waste pipe.

Figure 106   Fitting a waste outlet

Clearing stoppages in waste pipes

Choked waste pipes may be cleared either by the application of suction and pressure, or by using wires or canes. Where compressed air is available it may be used to bring direct pressure to bear in clearing stoppages.

Suction and pressure

Force cups and force pumps are used for creating suction and pressure on stoppages in waste pipes.

Figure 107   Clearing a stoppage in a waste pipe

Force cups

A stoppage in a single fixture may be cleared by using a force cup, as shown in Figure 107. A force cup consists of a rubber cup with a wooden handle, and is placed over the outlet of the fixture and worked with a reciprocating action, thus causing suction and pressure in the waste pipe. Force cups are particularly useful for stoppages in lavatory basins.

Force pumps

A patent force pump with a rubber cup and a pump attached is also used for waste pipework.

22

Home Improvement Grants

Over two million older homes have been modernized, mainly in respect of bathroom facilities, with the aid of home improvement grants since the system was introduced in 1949.

But many homes still lack basic amenities. In fact, it has been estimated that there are over a million homes in England without a bath, let alone an inside w.c.

Assistance for people who want to improve and modernize older homes in sound condition was increased by the Housing Act, 1969. The main obstacle, however, is a lack of knowledge by the general public of just what they are entitled to under the grants and how they go about getting it.

There are four types of grant available through local councils: improvement grants; intermediate grants; repairs grants; and special grants.

Grants are intended to help repair, improve, or provide with basic amenities homes which were built before 1961 (or, in the case of repairs, before 1919).

There are, of course, conditions and limits on the amounts payable. They may be granted to owner-occupiers, landlords and tenants, and full details can be obtained from your local town hall.

The maximum amounts of the grants and conditions are set in May each year by the Department of the Environment and local authorities base their figures on these. The amount of grant you are likely to receive depends on the amount of work you want to do, where you live, and what sort of work is needed. The council will decide whether or not to give you a grant, and how much. The table below gives rough guidance for a typical year.

Improvement grants are intended to improve homes to a good standard or to provide additional homes through conversions. They are discretionary and are normally paid at 50 per cent of eligible expenses (total cost of agreed works which may include professional services).

Intermediate grants are to help meet the cost of providing missing basic amenities – fixed bath or shower, washbasin, sink, hot- and cold-water supply to each, and a w.c., which should normally be inside the dwelling. These grants are mandatory.

Repair grants are available only for houses or flats built before 1919 to cover major structural repairs: roof, walls, floors, foundations. They do not cover maintenance work such as rewiring or replacement of worn fixtures.

Special grants are not available to tenants. They are provided for basic improvements and the provision of means of escape from fire in houses in multiple occupation. Repairs and special grants are both discretionary unless the council has served a notice under Section 9 of the Housing Act 1957 for the former, or a notice under Section 15 of the Housing Act 1961, or Schedule 24 of the Housing Act 1980 for the latter, in which case a grant payment is mandatory.

As a result of grant aid the condition of the property must be brought up to a standard acceptable to the council and have a further useful life of at least thirty years. Rateable value must not be more than £400 in Greater London or £225 elsewhere. This figure is increased in certain cases, such as home improvement grants, and as stated above, figures quoted here are typical. Check the current figures.

The following table sets out the limits for eligible expenses and the percentage rate normally paid. It must be understood that the totals shown are not the total payable grants but the cash limit set on work agreed to be done. Any costs over and above these limits must be met from your own resources.

If the property is in need of structural repair, intermediate grants may also include a repairs element of up to £4200 in Greater London and £3000 elsewhere.

A higher percentage (65 per cent) is payable on improvement grants if the property is in a general improvement area.

	*Typical amounts**				
	In Greater				*Priority*
Grant	*London*	*Elsewhere*	*%*	*London*	*Elsewhere*
Improvement	£ 9000	£6600	50**	£13,800	£10,200
Intermediate	£ 3005	£2275	90		
Repairs	£ 6600	£4800	90		
Special					
Means of escape	£10,800	£8100	50		
Repairs element	£ 4200	£3000	90		
Standard Amenities					
– depends on number					
needed			90		

* Check the current level of grants at your town hall: they change from time to time and almost certainly yearly.

** An extra 25 per cent is payable for priority improvement (houses in particularly bad condition, unfit, lacking standard amenities, or in need of substantial structural repair) for which increased eligible expenses are allowed as shown in the right-hand columns.

Help for the disabled

Grants for work to adapt houses for the accommodation, welfare, or employment of a disabled person are available at the highest (priority) rates on all grants and there are no rateable-value limits.

If you are applying for grant aid it is important not to start any work before your grant is approved by the council.

Grant approval is not the same as building or drainage approval; the appropriate departments of the local authority must be contacted for these approvals and any necessary drawings and forms submitted.

Grants are not available for second, or holiday, homes. On receiving the grant you will be required to give an undertaking to occupy the premises for five years. You can sell the house to another owner-occupier for him and his family to occupy or, after the first year, you can let it, but if it is used in any other way within five years after the work is finished the council may demand that the grant, or part of it, is repaid with interest.

Grants for insulation of buildings are separate from and in addition to those listed above.

Index